GIVING
THE BABY
BACK

Finding motherhood through

Infertility, foster care, and adoption

Daffodil Campbell

©2013

Thanks to everyone who encouraged my writing.

I am so grateful

~

This book is dedicated

to all of the children I have been lucky enough to care for

to Max and Lucy, my favorite and my best

to Sarah, who made it happen

to Rebecca, who showed me how

And most of all to my Sam,

who knew I could do it, and held my hand

"What lies behind us and what lies before us

are small matters compared to what lies within us."

-Ralph Waldo Emerson

~many of the details in this book have been altered to protect privacy~

Table of Contents

Prologue: The Cold Hard Truth

I wanted another baby desperately.

I wish that I could say that my husband and I became foster parents because we felt some sort of calling, or for the greater good, or because the situation presented itself and we stepped in and took a parentless child into our home. But the bottom line is, we wanted another baby. Okay, *I* wanted another baby.

I needed another baby.

We had emerged victorious from a difficult first pregnancy, and we weighed all of the options for child number two – reluctantly, I might add. All around us, people were breeding like rabbits. First, second, even third children were being conceived purposefully, accidentally, and everywhere in-between. But not for us. Never for us. I gave up education and employment, opportunities and experiences - my entire adult life, in fact, had been devoted to the pursuit of motherhood.

Eventually we discussed the possibility of adopting a child. Opening ourselves up to the idea of adoption was very difficult. At first it was as though we were admitting defeat. And we had other concerns: bonding with an adopted child, and whether we would feel differently parenting an adopted child vs. our biological son. Whether there would be a relationship with the birth parents. Then there was the question of finances: while we had good jobs and owned our own home and two reliable cars, the costs associated with adoption can be daunting. There is also the very real possibility that even after paying for the birth mother's living and medical expenses, and hiring a lawyer, that the biological mother could reconsider. It seemed incredibly risky.

And then we learned more about foster care. We knew about foster care in general, of course, but in my mind it had never really been an option – until suddenly, it was. Foster care would not include any significant financial burden, just our time and our love – of which we had plenty. There was very little chance of adopting a newborn foster child, but it didn't seem as far-fetched as a private adoption when we considered our budget. And so we began foster parenting on the "foster-to-adopt" track. Little did I know that, even after adopting a child, we would continue to foster parent. For the past ten years we have welcomed children into our home for days, weeks, or months at a time. Each case has been unique, and each child has been a cherished member of the family for as long as they were living in our home. As the years have passed, we have narrowed our focus a bit, and now we only foster newborn infants, usually drug exposed, and most of the time only a few days old when they are brought to us.

The only goal I had for writing this book was to further the understanding of how many ways there are to become a parent, illustrate how difficult the path to parenthood can be no matter which route you take, and most importantly, to encourage others to consider foster parenting – or at least, to give everyone who reads this an honest reflection of our involvement with the program. I am not going to sugar coat anything. By going into foster parenting hoping to adopt, I probably became a foster parent for the wrong reasons. But I continue to foster because I have come to understand how valuable the experience is for everyone involved.

The decision to foster has affected our family in ways I could never have imagined. We have learned that there is a time to be selfless, and there can be a time to be selfish as well. We are reminded that every life has meaning and that compassion does, actually, have its limits. And most of all, we have learned that every child is a gift without measure – even if the gift is only ours to treasure for a short time.

Chapter 1 Hearty New England Stock

From a very young age, I always planned to be a mother – and never considered any sort of career or long-term plan other than having children and caring for them. Looking back now, it seems like a very conservative, "traditional family values" approach to life, and I can assure you that is definitely not the case. I come from a large, traditional family, yes. But they are not conservative, nor are they the model of so-called "family values".

The traditions, however, ran strong. My father was one of a long family legacy of newspaper editors in a medium-sized town in New England, and my mother was raising the kids and running the house – it was, to be sure, a very traditional two-parent family in the late 70s and early 80s, when many of my parents' generation were ditching tradition. Mom and Dad married right out of high school and had three kids before they were 30. Each of my parents had numerous siblings, and most of the relatives lived nearby. As a result, we were surrounded by a veritable herd of cousins. Fertility was a given, and we had a wave of new cousins born every two years or so. I had little exposure to adoption, and knew absolutely nothing about foster care. I lived in a world where children were produced on a regular basis following a predictable schedule about a year after the wedding, and toddled off to preschool just around the time the next one showed up.

Embracing their straight-out-of-a-50s-sitcom reality, Dad worked in the family business and Mom stayed home to drive the station wagon and do volunteer work. It was a life filled with beautiful homes in picturesque towns, big family parties on holidays, ski trips and vacations and private schools and lots of Laura Ashley dresses and Brooks Brother's suits. My parents made sure we had a roof over our heads in the right neighborhood, good food on the table, and excellent schools to educate us. And in turn, we stayed on a pretty well-defined path: we were all bright and accomplished students, who stayed out of any real trouble and made an excellent impression. During the middle of my junior year of high school, my father moved away to run a small newspaper in the tropics that had been purchased by the family years before and was languishing. Dad found that he loved island life and playing the role of erudite ex-pat, wandering through town in his batik shirts, rumpled linen pants and horn-rimmed glasses. Aside from brief visits home to New England once a month, he never came back.

As I approached my senior year of high school, my classmates were all discussing SAT scores and college applications. I wasn't interested. I had been dating the same guy for several years, and was more concerned with our future as a couple than with any future of my own. Rather than head off to the Ivy Leagues with the rest of my cousins as was expected of us, I still dreamed of having children and being a wife and mother. Much to the chagrin of my high school's career counselor and all of my college prep teachers, I had not a single career goal. My parents seemed unconcerned; I certainly was never given the opportunity to consider traveling abroad after high school or working an internship with a family friend somewhere, or doing anything, really, that might have broadened my horizons. I suggested that maybe I should put off attending college, but my father wouldn't hear of it. My mother accompanied me to a "Financial Aid" night at school, where they talked about loans and grants and scholarships. Overwhelmed by the information and wholly uninspired to begin with, we left early. I half-heartedly applied to a few state schools, the only requirement being that they were located near ski resorts. That might give you some sense of my dedication to higher learning. I was accepted by several, chose one, and declared myself a fashion design major based on years of working retail but with little consideration of my minimal artistic talents. It didn't matter – the fashion design program was somehow a part of the university's College of Agriculture, and they had not required a portfolio of any kind.

An engagement ring appeared a few months before graduation, which my teachers unanimously greeted with dismay and my parents accepted reluctantly. Despite the fact that my boyfriend also had minimal skills – life or employment – no goals beyond getting a case of beer for his day off, and a high school education, we were convinced that together we would make a happy future for ourselves. College was something I was doing to pass the time – and the rural upstate university was certainly not the place to be if you wanted to get ahead in the fashion industry. But it was a great place to find cheap rent and raise a family of snowboarders.

The night of my high school graduation, my father was notably absent. He was on deadline at the newspaper and couldn't get away. My mother and brothers and a few relatives gathered for dinner at a local restaurant after the ceremony, and as soon as the bill was paid I got in my car with my boyfriend and headed north to our newly-leased apartment - the car packed to the roof and my cat hiding under the back seat. A few weeks later my mother and brothers also left home – they moved down to the Caribbean to join my father. I would never have admitted it, but the fact that my own father didn't attend my high school graduation was a huge shove out of the nest – one I had been begging for…..but still. And having everyone promptly leave town meant I had no one to go home to if things didn't turn out as happily ever after as I had planned. It was sink or swim time, and all I had to keep me afloat was a brand new high school diploma, and a check for $7,000 – a settlement from a car accident a few months prior - which almost covered the cost of one semester of college.

That first semester was exactly as I had predicted: a total waste of time and money. I didn't care about my studies, and had no interest in a career – I wanted a baby. Maybe a career would have been a wiser choice, but I was determined to settle down and start a family. A simple plan - or so I thought. It turned out that something so "simple" was going to be a lot more complicated - and expensive – than I had planned. But during those halcyon days between high school and the rest of my life, I truly believed that if I married my high school boyfriend and got an apartment and settled down, a baby would be practically inevitable.

So we unpacked, stocked the kitchen, found jobs, bought snow tires, and after a few conversations about how great it would be to have a baby right away, we ditched the birth control and started having a lot romantic conversations about whether the baby would be a boy or a girl. There was also a lot of drinking, which was our familiar routine from high school. Now that we were on our own with no "adult supervision" we did exactly as we pleased. When we weren't trying to get me pregnant, I worked almost every day – a schedule that was manageable during the summer. But once classes began it quickly became almost impossible to keep up. The bunk in my mandatory freshman dorm room that I was going to have to pay for eventually (though we still hadn't discussed how, exactly) sat empty. I went from home to class to work, leaving at 7am and returning at 9pm or later. I was exhausted and in way over my head. The stress left me feeling completely drained each day - or at least I thought it was stress. In mid-October, I discovered I was nine weeks pregnant.

I was thrilled. Briefly.

At my follow-up ultrasound appointment the next week, I was informed gravely that the pregnancy was not progressing normally, and the spotting I was experiencing was probably the beginning of a miscarriage. The size of the fetus was "off". They ordered some bloodwork, and when I returned for the results and a follow up

14

ultrasound I was advised that there were two options: I could let this pregnancy run its course – which no one encouraged me to do - or I could have a procedure they referred to as a "d and c". When I mentioned it to a co-worker, she said "That's an abortion." She then proceeded to tell me about her own abortion experience, while I stood in shocked silence. The clinic never called it an abortion, but rather a "procedure" and in retrospect, I wonder why. As an 18 year old patient in a college town, I am sure the doctors assumed my pregnancy was an accident, and clearly my co-worker did too. I was truly bewildered when my fiancé seemed to think the same thing. He told me in no uncertain terms that it wasn't the right time to have a baby, and his rejection left me in a stunned daze of fatigue, emotions, and hormones.

The appointment for a d and c was scheduled.

Devastated, I sat at home watching TV and crying. I ate nothing but chocolate chip cookies with M&M's, and would lie in bed for hours staring at the ceiling of our bedroom. A friend from school came and sat on the bed one afternoon, assuring me over and over again that it just wasn't meant to be this time. I tried to hold on to that, but even though I had only been a few months pregnant, and only known about the pregnancy for a few days, it felt as though a child - my child - had been taken away from me. I was empty and broken. I stopped attending classes altogether for a few weeks, started seeing a therapist, and applied for a medical withdrawal from school. It was denied, and so I struggled to return to class and catch up, while working at night to pay for tuition. The lowest point was the evening I took that third job:

I knew I was making a decision right then to drop out of college. I was now working six or seven days a week, and my class projects slipped by the wayside. All of the money I was earning would go to pay for tuition that would never benefit me. The fact that I was dropping out of school to sit in a phone bank each night calling people with telephone surveys was just….. it was unbelievable. Soon there were three foot snowdrifts outside. It would be completely dark by late afternoon. It was freezing cold, and incredibly depressing. I felt helpless. Hopeless. This – none of this – was what I had planned.

When I look back on that winter, I can see that the end of that pregnancy – the baby I had only known about for a few days – was the beginning of my undoing. I would sit at the telephone polling company, continuously reflecting back on all of the decisions I had made since that day at the clinic, all of the choices that brought me to that windowless room, and the cubicle with nothing but a computer and a telephone. I could have had it all, and instead I had nothing.

And so in those very sad days of winter, I came to believe that a baby would make everything better. My dream of becoming a mother shifted from something I wanted, to something I needed. There was a desperation that came with the need - a void I was desperately trying to fill. There was, of course, one problem with this: clearly, I needed to get my fiancé on board first. I had been so stunned when he seemed surprised that having unprotected sex had led to a pregnancy. We had spent many an hour planning to have a child, and I didn't understand why he had been anything but excited when the test had come back positive. Rather than have a conversation about it, I convinced myself that he had just been trying to be supportive in the face of a possible miscarriage. He would feel differently the next time, when the pregnancy was a healthy one. I had gotten pregnant easily, and I would get pregnant again - and he would be as excited as I was. He certainly didn't start wearing condoms, or show any concern in that regard. As the darkness and cold crept over us every afternoon, we returned to our familiar pattern – working and drinking and sleeping our way through the winter. By the end of February I was truly depressed and, despite my best efforts, not pregnant.

We decided on impulse to go visit my parents in the Caribbean, and get married while we were there. We spent the week meeting everyone in town and being convinced by my father to move down to the island permanently and work at the paper. I returned to New England's slush and muddy snow with a gorgeous bouquet of stargazer lilies to dry in my overheated apartment, and a new plan. In short order, we packed up, drove to Florida, shipped the car, and flew south. The winter had been hard on me physically and emotionally, and I welcomed the change. Since I had dropped out of school, there was nothing tying us to that college town anymore. And living there, we were far from our future children's grandparents, who would be providing all of that free babysitting I assumed we would be needing shortly.

In retrospect, perhaps we moved *too* close. Having a bedroom across the hall from my brothers' room and next to my father's office put an immediate damper on the baby-making activities. But we were young and in love, and even with a "too close for comfort" living situation, we still managed to find time alone. We were living in paradise, for free, and we had our whole lives ahead of us. My husband was drinking more with each passing week, and working sporadically. I was working at the paper during the day, and waiting tables at night.

As time went on, and despite our clandestine attempts, I still did not get pregnant. I wasn't worried – I had gotten pregnant quite by accident in the past, and I assumed that it would happen again without too much effort. And then one night I awoke suddenly, bent double with stabbing pain in my stomach. I tried to get out of bed and collapsed onto the cold tile, writhing, muffling my screams with the edge of the comforter. My husband, meanwhile, was in a panic – and probably still drunk from dinner. He was scrambling around in the dark shouting "Where ARE you? What is going on?" He managed to find a light switch and came to kneel next to me on the floor.

For hours, we lay in the dark. First next to the bed, and eventually I was able to crawl back up to the mattress. I curled into a tight ball, and rocked back forth, whimpering. There was no 911 system, no way to summon help, and no help to be summoned. So we waited for dawn, and tried to make a plan.

The next day we started off to the small island clinic that was still under construction, where they gave me a prescription for pain medication and sent me by ferry to another island, to see another doctor. I arrived at that appointment still in my pajamas, my hair sticky with salt water from a particularly rough channel crossing, and my eyes swollen from hours of crying. I was horrified when this doctor insisted on testing me for chlamydia. "I have only had sex with one person" I said indignantly. "And we have been together for four years. We are *married*. I do NOT have chlamydia."

The doctor looked at me disdainfully. "You don't know everything your husband does in his free time."

In my narcotic haze, I took that to mean that she *did* know, and when my husband met me at the ferry dock that afternoon – still in my pajamas and now, after a second ferry ride and another few hours of crying, looking pretty ragged - the entire crowd was treated to me accusing him of giving me the clap. It was not my finest moment, but it was certainly entertaining for those at the end of the gangplank – with the possible exception of my husband. He insisted that actually, I did indeed know everything that he did in his free time, and suggested that we get a second opinion. A few days later, we flew to Puerto Rico to see another doctor.

The building was older and chickens scattered as we approached the door. The groaning, halting elevator had us looking for the stairs, and the windowless waiting room was packed with patients – hugely pregnant women, their partners and children surrounding them, sometimes also accompanied by what I assumed were the grandparents to-be. Every patient seemed to have at least four other people with her, and they all spoke loudly as they read battered copies of Spanish language gossip magazines. I made my way through the chaos to the desk, only to discover that the receptionist did not speak English. We did not speak Spanish. I showed her my ID, she checked us off the list, and I was able to decipher the registration paperwork with some educated guesses, relying heavily on my 10 years of French classes. Then we sat back to wait. The loud voices, the foreign words I didn't understand, the kids running everywhere, all illuminated by the green hue of the fluorescent lights and a flickering TV – it was surreal. Still on heavy doses of pain medication, I was terrified. There had been CHICKENS outside the building. I couldn't understand a word anyone was saying to me. The office was run down, and I was sure the doctor was going to be some old, creepy guy with a headlamp and a rusty speculum. This was not what I had in mind. I longed for the quiet suburban OB/GYN office in New England, with its burbling fish tank and current issues of Vogue and the comfy couches, where patients spoke in hushed tones and avoided eye contact.

Eventually we were ushered back, down a narrow hallway and into a small exam room. It was clean, and blessedly quiet. I lay down on the cool paper and closed my eyes. I opened them when the doctor arrived. There was no head lamp in sight – Dr. Castillo was a handsome man, in his mid-thirties. He had returned to Puerto Rico after attending medical school in the States, and most importantly, he spoke English. I almost cried in relief. Someone finally seemed to know what was going on, and would be able to explain it to me without a translator. He ordered an ultrasound, and we dutifully walked around the corner to yet another decrepit building and dark waiting room, where I didn't understand a word that people said to me. Films and report in hand, we returned to Dr. Castillo's office, and sat across from him, waiting to hear the results. And that is when we discovered that I did not have a biological clock - I had a biological time bomb. He could see a massive cyst, and suspected one had already ruptured that night when the pain had been so terrible.

Surgery confirmed that I had endometriosis and ovarian cysts. The cyst that ruptured had been large, and the damage to my ovary was significant – only time would tell how my body would recover. The diagnosis was both a relief and a warning: I knew now why I wasn't getting pregnant, but I also knew that it was not going to be quite as easy as I had expected. That knowledge both drove me and dragged me towards motherhood - I was unwilling to consider a life without children, and now that I knew children might not come easily, getting pregnant had become a quest.

A few weeks after the surgery we returned to the doctor's office, and he showed me photos and diagrams of what we were dealing with. We were also treated to a particularly gruesome video of my own surgery, which left me wincing and my husband looking sort of pale and sweaty. As we were getting ready to leave the doctor leaned forward and said "If you want to have biological children, I suggest you get serious about it." So we went down the street and bought a thermometer, and armed with his instructions and a handful of brochures on the science of conception, we got very, very serious.

It turned out that trying to get pregnant was not a lot of fun when the pressure was on. Living with my parents was not helping matters. My husband's drinking was another roadblock. And then one night at work, as I watched the sun set on the horizon from the entrance to the restaurant, I saw someone that looked just like my husband, in a car that looked just like mine, driving past with another woman in the passenger seat. I was horrified. I called him on his cellphone and told him that I had seen him. What was he thinking? Where was he going? A short time later he staggered up the stairs and leaned against the hostess stand. He was drunk. He denied everything, and then argued with the bartender. I was sent home early and told in no uncertain terms by the manager to take my belligerent spouse with me.

The fight that happened late that night was……extraordinary. My father and younger brother intervened. There were threats and a baseball bat was brandished. In the morning I bought my husband a plane ticket back to our home town, and he moved in with his grandmother.

We tried to make it work. I followed him back and we lived in a series of tiny apartments while I waited tables and cleaned houses. I still didn't get pregnant – though why we continued to have unprotected sex while our marriage was falling to pieces is hard to explain. The marriage faltered, and then crumbled. Within six months we had separated and found new partners to distract ourselves with; our divorce was finalized just after my 21st birthday. I sat in the bedroom I now shared with another man, and stared at the court documents in my lap. I cried, and I grieved, and then I resolved to get my shit together and clear the slate. A fresh start. I disappeared one rainy night with no warning, hopping a plane back to the Caribbean. And still, the clock was ticking.

Chapter 2 Naturally Unnatural

My quest to get pregnant did not end with my marriage. As a newly single woman – one who had never dated as an adult, and had married her first serious boyfriend – I jumped into dating with both feet and no parachute. Surprisingly, when they heard my story plenty of men volunteered to "help out". Armed with my trusty thermometer I let a few of them take a crack at it - with disappointing results. I wasn't quite sure what to do next – was I supposed to give up on having a baby, and go back to school? I still had no career goal, and I was happy waitressing. Days slipped by as I lay on the beach all day with my co-workers and friends (none of whom had any long term plans other than which bar they were heading to that night). Evenings found me hosing off in the parking lot behind the restaurant, before tying an apron around my waist and gong to work at 5pm. Eventually, I decided that if I was going to actually *get* my shit together, I should probably find a better place to do it than surrounded by people who were intentionally avoiding responsibility. I moved to Boston, bought a suit and a pair of heels, got a job as an office manager for an international engineering firm, and stepped into the rat race. I had steady work with benefits, a new boyfriend with an even better job than my own, and I settled in to my new "grownup" life. This was it. I was on my way.

Except, the job bored me to tears. So did the guy. And I still wasn't getting pregnant. In fact, in the year I was in Boston, I had surgery twice and suffered through another miscarriage – one that began as I sat for hours on an Amtrak train broken down in the middle of nowhere. The endometriosis was advancing, and my fertility was dwindling as the scar tissue slowly twisted its way around my abdomen. The ticking of the clock had advanced to a deafening, mind-numbing metronome – and it was speeding up. I felt completely out of control of my own body, and I was totally, utterly miserable in general. I quit the job and got a new one, which helped. And when he informed me solemnly that he didn't want to get married because I might not be able to have biological children, I broke up with the guy and moved in with Stacey, a girlfriend I had met at work. I tried, for a moment, to just focus on living my life, and not creating a new one.

But I couldn't shake it. I still went through every day wishing I had a partner and a child. I would hold other people's babies greedily, not wanting to give them back, happily changing even the scariest of diapers and gleefully wiping spit-up off my clothes. Every pregnant belly and baby carriage was a reminder of what I did not have. It also became clear that I was terrible at dating. Going to the clubs with my roommate was not how I wanted to spend my evenings. I had an unpredictable work schedule so it was impossible to sign up for classes or commit to anything on a regular basis, even a date. And still, the idea of being single, going back to school, forgetting about having a baby for a while – those thoughts were dismissed as soon as they entered my mind. I remained completely focused on becoming a mother, and every roadblock I came across just deepened my resolve. When I think back on it now, I wish I had directed that passion towards a cause greater than my uterus, but I guess there are lots of 22 year olds who are pretty self-absorbed. I can say this with certainty: no 22 year old should be trying to figure out her life and her fertility at the same time. It's impossible. Most people that age can barely manage to keep toilet paper in the house.

And then, as these things happen, I got totally blind-sided.

I met a man who did not want to get married, or have children – but strangely enough, he wanted me. He was Stacey's cousin, a "confirmed bachelor" as my grandmother would say.

Sam was older, owned his own home, had a career and a life and a plan. A plan that did not involve a family. He had long hair and a dozen guitars, and tie-dyed blackout curtains in his bedroom. He was not looking to settle down, and so I was very clear with him. I gave him the whole story. I explained to him that I was on a quest to have a child while I still could. That being with me meant getting me pregnant – as soon as possible. I had my third surgery right after we met, and had been warned again that time was taking its toll. We were friends, and there was no point in avoiding the subject: I didn't want to waste his time, and I didn't have any time to waste. I wasn't going to get pregnant accidentally, or secretly. I knew from experience that this was going to take a concerted effort, and some very careful scheduling. The doctors had already broached the scary-sounding topic of "assisted reproductive technology" - which sounded a lot more complicated than thermometers. I wasn't going to casually date someone - I had a mission. Finally covered by health insurance and earning a steady income, I needed one last detail: sperm. I was turned off by the anonymity of a sperm bank. I wanted to know the man who would be my child's father, and because I had the feeling it was going to take a few tries, I wanted to make sure my "donor" was willing to stick around long enough for a healthy birth. I didn't need a partner to parent my child, but I did need a partner to become a parent. And so I sat across from Sam at dinner one night, and laid it all on the table. He wasn't thrilled with the conversation, but he understood and respected my honesty. We parted that evening reluctantly, as friends.

A few days later my phone rang at work.

"I need to talk to you." he said.

"About what?" I asked. I was at the register of the boutique I was managing at the time, and there was a line winding its way through the store. I tucked the phone under one ear and waved the next customer forward.

"I thought that I didn't want to get married and have kids. I mean, I didn't want to get married and have kids. But I changed my mind." His words tumbled over themselves.

I stopped scanning tags and stood there for a minute trying to understand what he was trying to say. "Changed your mind about what?" I was confused.

"I want to marry you, and have a baby with you. Let's get married and have a baby." He was totally calm now. I stood there with my mouth hanging open, staring at the cash drawer that had just popped open.

"Um. I'm sorry. What?"

"I took a long walk on the beach, and I talked to my dad about it. He said the best thing he ever did was get married and have kids. And I realized – he's right. It will be great. I just hadn't met the right person yet." Why was he so calm?

I shook my head. "YOU TALKED TO YOUR *DAD*?"

"Yep." He sounded almost smug. This was so bizarre.

"Can we go out on a date first?"

"Sure. Yes. Absolutely. Then we can get married. And then we can have a baby."

And so we did. Six months later we were married on a beach in front of a cheering crowd of family and friends, and we settled into married life with a plan to get serious and start a family by any means necessary. If Sam had any notion that having a baby was going to be fun, or romantic, or easy, well......he saw the cold hard truth on one of the countless exam tables I found myself sprawled across. The first time he sat next to me while my feet were in stirrups and a doctor was twisting an ultrasound wand around between my legs, I am pretty sure he wanted to crawl under the table and die. It was an endless stream of procedures and days of appointments with one specialist after another. I saw doctors and surgeons, naturopaths and acupuncturists, faith healers and massage therapists. I swallowed, swabbed, injected, sucked and absorbed anything that was handed to me in my single-minded pursuit of a child. My days passed in a haze of fertility drugs, my body covered in bruises from the daily injections. By my mid-twenties, we had shelled out thousands of dollars to pay for the procedures and drugs required to conceive our son. And I wasn't sure when to throw in the towel. Should we keep trying, spending money on treatments that might be better saved to fund an adoption, until we had exhausted all options – and finances? Was there ever going to be a time when I would have to give up due to a bankruptcy – financial or emotional? We were lucky to have most of my treatment covered by medical insurance, and I knew we couldn't afford adoption so I never wavered – if a doctor told me to try a new medication or procedure, I was game. There always seemed to be another step to take along the path to biological parenthood.

One Sunday morning we were at the doctor's office for an ultrasound to measure my uterine lining or my follicles or something else ridiculously clinical. These clinics are open seven days a week because "ovaries don't rest on Sundays" a nurse cheerfully informed me when scheduling the appointment. So there we were on a Sunday morning in March, and I found myself flipping through magazines next to a woman who was perched on the very edge of her seat, clutching her purse with both hands. She sat, straight-backed, waiting for her name to be called. This was their last cycle, she told me. Her face was strained, her voice emotionless. They had mortgaged the house, she explained, and this was their very last chance. They were out of money, and out of options. She was so matter-of-fact about it, and as she spoke I sat there wondering how far I would have to go to have a child. I willed myself to focus on a positive end result, as the nurses had suggested. "Don't go negative" I chanted to myself silently. Sam saw the look of panic on my face, had taken my hand and squeezed it. It might not sound romantic, but in the midst of a very unromantic process, it was the best he could do. If we were going down, we were going down together.

Chapter 3 Maternal Instincts

I was told by well-meaning but very detached medical professionals that intrauterine inseminations (IUIs) are the last step before the much more invasive - and expensive - in-vitro fertilization (IVF). At this point, having sex – actual sex for fun or for procreation – was discouraged. Everything needed to be charted and accounted for. And after in-vitro, we would talk about surrogates, unless a better option came along. As I was trudging through the process of getting pregnant, science was, thankfully, always one step ahead. Every time I went in to be scanned, poked, prodded or otherwise assessed, the nurses would reassure me that there were still plenty of options and many reasons to be hopeful. While the process of getting pregnant through reproductive science may not be a romantic one, it can be very efficient. With my young eggs and Sam's (by all accounts) spectacular sperm count, and a technique called a "double IUI" where they inseminated me two days in a row, we were finally successful. The entire experience – start to finish – had been one of cool detachment and scientific odds. In the end, it turned out that Sam was working in another city the day I got pregnant. I lay alone in the clinic on crinkly paper, being inseminated by a lovely nurse named Heather. I sent her a thank you card afterwards.

Once again, the early blood tests and ultrasounds of my pregnancy were worrisome. At least no one brought up having a "procedure". But the numbers were low. The size was that all too familiar "off". They hesitated to even confirm that I was pregnant for the first two months while they waited for my condition – such as it was – to stabilize. But finally the measurements and numbers and heart rate caught up with the calendar, and they released me to the care of a midwife - wishing me well and encouraging me to send photos when the baby was born.

We went directly to the store to buy a crib and start planning the nursery. I let my worries dissolve and celebrated being finally, fully pregnant. But the passing days showed me that, like everything else I had experienced relating to childbearing, nothing about my pregnancy was going to be easy.

First came the mind-numbing fatigue. It hit its peak at about 10 weeks. One afternoon I lay down on the bed and tossed the cordless phone next to me on the mattress. I have no idea how much time passed, but at some point the phone began to ring. I lay there and opened one eye, unmoving. The phone was, at most, a foot away from my hand. And yet, the thought of moving to answer it was impossible to consider. I could not so much as raise a finger off the mattress. I lay there and stared at the phone ringing, wishing it would stop so I could go back to sleep in peace.

And then there was the nausea. I spent 50% of my day standing over a garbage can, toilet, shrub, gutter, plastic bag, box, or anything else I could get my hands on, debating whether I was going to puke or not – and wishing that I could just get it over with. I would try to go grocery shopping, but the entire store smelled like the meat department: a refrigerated case that stood at the end of every aisle, and extended the length of the back wall of the store.

I had been rather thin to begin with when we conceived. The stress had taken its toll, and the fertility drugs had made me nauseous – I dropped 10 pounds in the months before I got pregnant, and now the constant nausea of early pregnancy was keeping me underweight. However, as the pounds continued to slip off my frame, my stomach began to swell and distend as the baby – "the parasite" as Sam began to call it – continued to grow.

And then, of course, there were the mood swings. I cried with very little provocation, and it only got worse when I learned that I actually had something to cry about.

A routine ultrasound was scheduled at 21 weeks. This was the big fun ultrasound where you get to see your baby sucking it's thumb and find out the sex of your unborn child (as long as the baby cooperates). I was beyond excited, and Sam and I were both anxious to find out if I was having a boy or a girl so that we could decide on a name. I invited my mother along, and she met us early in the morning at the hospital. We sat in the waiting room reading pregnancy magazines until the tech called us back to a small dim room with nothing more than an exam table and a monitor. When she placed the wand on my belly, her first question was "And do we want to know the sex?"

"Yes!" The answer was unanimous and we all craned our necks to get a better view. The tech worked silently, taking measurements and photos as we tried to discern what – exactly – we were looking at. She zoomed in and out, moved the wand from one side of my belly to the other with such speed that I had motion sickness. The photos came streaming out of the computer and finally she said "It's a boy!" She measured the defining organ, and then went back to work.

We were jubilant. As I lay there, we debated names and guessed how big he was – and how big he would be. After a while, the conversation died down, and we realized that the tech was still hard at work. There was a pile of paper at her feet and she was staring intently at the screen. "Boy, we sure are getting our money's worth!" I cracked. She didn't smile.

"Everything okay?" my mother asked.

The tech turned off the screen and ripped off the long stream of paper from the printer, gathering up the printout and turning towards the door. "I'll be right back" she called over her shoulder.

"Okaaaaaay…" I looked at Sam. "What was *that* all about?"

He shrugged and sat down on a nearby chair. "She probably has to take it to the radiologist. Or maybe she is bringing us back some photos to keep after she takes what she needs?"

The door opened again, and a woman in a white coat walked in, followed by the tech. She turned the monitor back on and grabbed the bottle of jelly, squeezing a blob out on my stomach without warning.

She introduced herself and grabbed the wand, turning to the monitor and getting to work.

"Did you have the triple screen?" she asked. The triple screen is a test for "flags" that would lead to more testing, mostly for genetic issues. Several of my friends had experienced many sleepless nights because of false positives on their test results. The last thing I needed was more tests, and more cause for concern. So I had opted out.

"No......why?"

She stopped moving the wand around and turned to me. "May I ask why not?"

"Because a bunch of my friends got false positives, and since this ultrasound was the next step if the results were questionable, I opted to just skip that test and go straight to the 3-d images. Why?"

"Well," she turned back to the screen. "We are seeing something abnormal."

That was the moment that I burst into tears. And for the first time in my pregnancy, there was a damn good reason. The images had revealed a birth defect – one kidney was abnormally large, and I would need to consult with a specialist. When the doctor and tech left the room, I lay on the table wiping off my belly and crying quietly. I looked over at my mother at one point and I remember saying "Mom, something is wrong with my baby. How could this happen?" But the fact is it happens a lot, actually. Three to four percent of all newborns have some sort of birth defect. This fun fact was shared with me by a genetic counselor who replaced the doctor and ultrasound tech, in an effort to help me calm down – which just made me more hysterical. Eventually the counselor gave up trying to talk to us and the doctor came back in, informing me that I needed to compose myself before I would be allowed to leave the room. They didn't want a waiting room full of hysterical pregnant women wondering if they were in the three percent, apparently. As I took deep breaths and mopped at my face, plans were made for further testing at birth. In the coming weeks, that birth threatened to take place well ahead of schedule.

The first time I went into labor I was alone in a movie theater watching a matinee. As Gwyneth Paltrow and Huey Lewis crooned on screen, I felt my entire midsection tighten. I caught my breath and shifted my weight in the seat. A few minutes later it happened again. And then again. I had slouched down until I was almost lying in the seat, my legs straddling the chair in front of me, both hands on my belly. I was almost six months pregnant.

The next time my muscles relaxed, I pulled myself to standing and staggered up the aisle. When I got out in the hallway I leaned up against the wall as another contraction hobbled me. I knew I was in trouble when I voluntarily decided to ease myself down onto that filthy floor. Searching through my bag, I found my cellphone and called my midwife. "I'm having contractions." I said breathlessly.

"You need to go to the hospital." She was serious. Very no nonsense, she had an air of calm control which I appreciated during my visits, and which was keeping me focused as I sat on the floor of the movie theater. "Call 911." She said. "You need to call 911."

The idea of being rolled through the mall on a stretcher was horrifying. Sam had steadfastly refused to get a cellphone, but I had talked him into carrying a pager when I got pregnant. I paged him. "911". Then I slowly made my way back to standing, and began a halting walk out to the car. There would be no ambulance. I was doing this on my own power, thanks.

20 minutes later Sam called me back. "What's going on? I'm on the highway in traffic, sorry it took forever to get to the next exit and I-"

"I'm in labor."

"What do you mean, you're in labor?"

"JUST COME GET ME WHAT THE HELL IS WRONG WITH YOU?" Another contraction was rolling in and I had a death grip on my purse as I shuffled along.

"WHERE ARE YOU?" he shouted back, totally freaked out.

"I'm at the movies." I was trying to find my car keys.

"WHAT?"

"I'm at the movies. I'm parked next to the pizza place."

"I'll be there in 20 minutes." The line went dead.

By the time he found my car in the parking lot, I was in the front passenger seat, reclined all the way back. "Park your car, babe. I am not getting out of this seat unless there is a wheelchair outside." I was breathing my way through another contraction.

"Right, got it." He slammed the door and disappeared, returning in a few minutes out of breath and sweating. We drove in silence. I gripped the door handle during contractions, he had the emergency flashers on as we swerved through traffic. The midwife called a few times to check our progress. "You should have called an ambulance!" she scolded me.

Once I was settled in the labor and delivery ward and they saw my contractions on the screen, I was admitted. They started a drip of something that stopped the contractions, and I had to spend the night for observation. I was sent home the next day, wobbly but pregnant. I was still pregnant and that was all that mattered.

 I had contractions pretty frequently after that, usually if I was tired or dehydrated, and six weeks before my due date I was hospitalized again in pre-term labor. This time, they decided to let me deliver. I was hooked up to monitors, given an IV, and observed. They started Pitocin to regulate my contractions and get things moving – which didn't happen. As night fell, I was sent home. Still pregnant, still contracting, but not dilated

And so, I remained steadfastly pregnant, with strong regular contractions, for two long months. For years I couldn't get pregnant, and now I couldn't wait to not be pregnant anymore. Prodromal labor, they called it. About a month before my due date the midwife informed me during my exam that the baby was big - probably about 8 pounds. "He'll be 8 pounds when he's born? That's not big…that's a totally norma-"

"No," she interrupted me as she took notes in my chart. "He's about 8 pounds right now."

"But I'm not due for another month!"

"I know. You might want to cut down on your juice intake."

"JUICE? I don't drink juice! That book you gave me said they gain half a pound a week during the last month. I do NOT want to have a 10 pound baby."

"Well, there's not much you can do about it. He's a big baby." She seemed unconcerned.

She didn't have to give birth to him. I was horrified.

I distracted myself from the impending delivery by focusing on finding a specialist to deal with the baby's enlarged kidney. I visited several doctors armed with film and notes from that awful ultrasound, and I settled on a wonderful pediatric nephrologist at the Boston Children's Hospital. I loved him. He was sweet and kind and calm. His staff was lovely and I liked the hospital too. We were lucky to live in a place where I had my choice not just of pediatric specialists, but pediatric hospitals as well. His office was across the street from the hospital where I would be delivering, and if anything was wrong he could be there in 10 minutes. I found that very reassuring, and at that point I was looking for reassurance where ever I could find it.

By the time I was finally admitted to labor and delivery (for good this time) I had been contracting regularly for almost eight weeks, and was at a "plus two" the midwife kept telling me. I had no idea what that meant, because apparently I wasn't dilated at all, but it *felt* like I had a bowling ball in my crotch. Someone suggested that Sam and I have sex to encourage labor and I told them (in somewhat less delicate terms) to have sex with themselves if it was so fantastic. Sam wasn't getting anywhere near me. I was a very cranky pregnant woman.

I rolled into the hospital a week overdue, carrying an extra 80 pounds on my frame, ready to be induced. Max's birth followed my usual pattern – parenthood had not come easily at any point, and the delivery itself was just a continuation of the nightmare. About 18 hours into the ordeal, I rolled over and asked Sam why, exactly, we had gone through so much trouble. "I'm never doing this again." I proclaimed.

And then came the pushing. For two hours, I pushed. I pushed on my back, on my side, on my hands and knees. I pushed quietly, I pushed with grunts, I pushed with deep exhalation of breath. I pushed hard and I pushed long. I pushed with one knee in the air, and then the other. I pushed hanging onto a bar that had weirdly appeared out of thin air suspended over my bed, and I pushed squatting and clutching the back of the bed for dear life.

Hemorrhoid, thy name is childbirth.

I was exhausted, sure. But more than that, I was sad. Once again, this was not happening the way it was "supposed to". Since the beginning of time, women have labored alone, in caves and fields and under trees. They have squatted on the ground, given birth, and then gone right back to work. And here I was, in a bed, with four people assisting me and my husband cheering me on, and I still couldn't get it done.

I was stuck. Exhausted. And really, really pissed off.

This baby had to come out.

"I think it's time to consider a cesarean" my midwife was leaning over the bedrail, as I clung on to it for dear life and panted, clutching one knee up to my chest.

I glared at her and reached out to hold the lapel of her white coat. "Get him *out of me*." I hissed as I pulled her close. "I don't care how you do it. If it was up to me, I would have had the cesarean two weeks ago."

He was finally born in the midst of a two hour cesarean section that turned into full-blown abdominal surgery with the removal of a whole lot of scar tissue and something akin to a tummy-tuck. I don't think we need to re-hash the gory details of the birth story, let's just say that at birth, Max weighed more than nine and a half pounds, and was two feet long.

He looked like a toddler.

I may not have done such a hot job with conception, pregnancy and delivery, but I was seriously good at growing things in my stomach.

I finally got to hold Max about three hours after they had first wheeled me into the operating room, and he was beautiful. I was obsessed with him, and if he was gone for a moment too long in the nursery, or if one of the constant stream of visitors held him too close, I would demand his return. Breastfeeding came easily, and the maternal instinct was strong. But I never forgot the years leading up to his arrival. I kept waiting for that moment where you forget the horrors of birth and just stare into your child's eyes and know it's all worth it. That moment never came. I wondered, again and again, why it had to be so difficult. I didn't think I loved him more, or was more grateful to have him, just because of what I had gone through. I started to feel angry. Angry that parenthood had been withheld from me for so long. Did I have some debt to pay? Did I have to earn it? Prove myself?

Whatever the reasons, whatever the cause, I had overcome. We left the hospital triumphantly, signing out two days early in our eagerness to put this whole messy business behind us and start our life together as a family.

Max's pediatrician had contacted the nephrologist after the birth as we had planned, but because Max was peeing normally our pediatrician wasn't concerned – so we weren't either. Thrilled that it wasn't an emergency situation, we embraced his casual attitude about the follow-up testing. That could happen later, apparently, and we were happy to put it off for as long as possible.

When Max was seven weeks old, we flew to Hawaii. We spent our days at the beach, and napping, and wandering narrow streets with Max sleeping in our arms. We talked about our plans for the future, and how relieved we were to be done with trying to get pregnant, and worrying about the baby. We came home rested and healed from the trauma.

The answering machine was loaded with messages, and I nursed Max as I jotted down notes from each call. "Hi there, this is Dr. C. I want to apologize, the message about your son's birth was filed by my secretary before I had a chance to read it and I just found a follow-up message here from your pediatrician. We need to see Max right away. He needs to be taking a daily dose of antibiotics to prevent kidney infection while we run some tests and see what is going on with the little – well, my goodness 9 ½ pounds, not so little is he! You can call my office and schedule an appointment, they are expecting your call. Thanks, see you soon."

I sat back. The vacation was over.

And so we were thrown back into a routine of testing, appointments, hospitals and waiting rooms. Max was a happy baby, and easy to soothe – the hours in the car passed with him soundly asleep for the most part. When they were sticking him with needles or inserting catheters he would breastfeed, which seemed to help him stay calm and relaxed no matter how painful the procedure.

With the test results in, Dr. C decided that surgery was unavoidable, and should not be delayed. The operation to remove one kidney and re-implant the ureter on the other kidney was scheduled for May 1st – until then we put it out of our minds as often as possible. The day of the operation we sat on the edge of our seat in the waiting room with a few other families who were also waiting for a bed in pre-op. When they called our name we entered a large room divided by curtains, and we were told to undress Max and take all of his belongings with us while he was in surgery. We sat there in the cold room, all three of us curled up on the gurney together, holding each other both for warmth and reassurance.

I heard the footsteps approaching, and heard Dr. C's voice. I closed my eyes and leaned my head against Sam's shoulder. The nurse checked Max's bracelet to confirm his name, and had us sign a few forms. Dr. C went over the plan for the surgery again. They would hook him up to a machine that would replace his kidneys during the surgery. Max would lie on his stomach and they would take out the enlarged kidney through an incision in his back. Then they would close up that incision and roll him over, and they would make an incision in his lower abdomen in order to fix the valve in the ureter connected to his healthy kidney. Then they would take him off the dialysis and insert a drain, and close him up. It would take several hours.

I nodded silently. Sam thanked him. And then the nurse reached for my baby.

As I watched them walk away down the hall and through the swinging doors marked "O R", I could see the lights and the shining metal trays, hear the beeping and the chatter. Max lifted his head off of the nurse's shoulder as the doors swung shut, realizing at the last minute that I was not following him. We both began to cry at the same moment, and as I silently gathered his things I heard him wailing from the operating rom. Sam took my hand and led me away.

We spent the next few hours in the waiting room. I was walking back and forth to the pumping suite – a room set up with industrial grade breast pumps and trays of glass bottles that I filled over and over again. It was the one thing I could do – my baby wasn't here with me right now, but he would be. And I was going to have plenty of milk for him.

When the nurse at the information desk finally called us over and told us we could go and see him in recovery, we almost ran down the hallway. He lay on a small gurney with sides that could raise up into a crib. He was attached to monitors, with tubes snaking out of his body. There was some blood soaking through a piece of gauze on his belly.

I froze.

"He's fine." Sam said quietly. "They said he did really well. Go say hi."

And at that moment I felt this relief. This joy. It was over. It was really over. For five months I had been waiting for that moment when I saw my baby and just forgot everything, put it all behind me, and known it was all worth it – and now, suddenly, I could. It was such a relief.

Max was in the hospital for five days. We drove home with a carload of friends following us, balloons bobbing around the backseat and the windows open to breath in that precious fresh air that had been in such short supply in the pediatric ward. It was springtime in New England, a beautiful sunny warm day. Trees were green, flowers were blooming, and we were free. Really, truly, finally free. We could do anything. Go anywhere. Max was fine. We were fine. Life. Was. Good. And life was about to change.

Within a year, we packed up our most treasured possessions and had an epic yard sale - we were moving to Hawaii.

Chapter 4 Grown Here Not Flown Here

For the first few years in Hawaii, we focused on moving into our dream home. Painting and updating and renovating, making it ours. When Max turned three I enrolled him in a nursery school, and suddenly I had a lot of free time on my hands. Inevitably, I started thinking about baby number two.

We were once again trying to get pregnant – and once again, it was not going well. There is a process to trying to conceive – and not the process you are thinking of. Of course, all of the same fundamentals are involved, but for insurance purposes you have to follow protocol. First you just stop preventing – since we had never prevented anything in the first place, that was easily done. Then you start charting temperatures and examining discharge, a process that was never particularly helpful in my case. Then – and only then – do they start The Testing. Sperm are counted, ovaries are examined, dye is cast through channels that should not be dyed in an attempt to "clear the cobwebs" (which is a lovely way to think of your reproductive system, I assure you). Then – and only then – do they prescribe the drugs and get serious.

We were still in the taking temperatures and watching the calendar stage of the game, but even at this point it was becoming clear that if our son was going to have a sibling, we were – at the very least – probably going to need another set of ovaries. Another womb was not out of the question. Since we were already in the Science Project area of conception, I had reverted to my comfort zone and totally detached from the process. I looked at everything with a clear, no-nonsense New Englander sensibility. I was looking at the bottom line. I wanted another child. I didn't want to leave us destitute, didn't want to squander my child's college fund and spend his childhood whacked out on fertility drugs, trying desperately to conceive child number two. I was not ovulating, and I needed to be reasonable. I needed to make a plan.

The idea of adoption was terrifying – not to mention financially daunting. To be honest, there was no way we could adopt unless we used every penny of our meager retirement account. And the horror stories of people paying for the adoption, only to have it fall apart in the end, leaving them broke and broken hearted….. It was a huge risk. I ran the numbers. I tightened our budget. I tried to start an "adoption fund", but the costs seemed impossible. It wasn't just the actual adoption – what scared me was paying for the birth mother's living expenses, which fluctuated wildly but were without a doubt on the high end here in Hawaii. There was no way to really predict how much it might cost. I didn't understand how couples could afford to adopt a child – never mind more than one. How did they manage to pay the bills, cover the mortgage, and still shell out $40,000 to some lawyer or adoption agency? Were these people all independently wealthy?

Because I could barely manage to save $400 - never mind $40,000.

And I didn't know if I would be able to stand waiting – maybe for years - in the hopes that someone would choose us out of a huge book of potential adoptive families. Trying to market ourselves as the perfect family to women we would probably never meet – taking photos, writing a biography, trying not to sound desperate when I was, above all else, completely desperate. Or flying to a foreign country and being handed a child of indeterminate origin, who had been in foster homes or orphanages, who might remember their biological family and may have been separated from them in less-than-ideal circumstances, hoping that despite all of that, they might, somehow, be able to bond with us in time.

And what about those foster homes? I saw the ad every week in the free newspaper that was distributed all over town. "Children in Need of Loving Homes" the headline said. "Become a Foster Parent". I was sitting in yet another doctor's waiting room, in the middle of yet another unsuccessful cycle when I finally picked up my phone and called the number. Theresa answered, and was calm, reassuring, but also realistic. Yes, foster parents were desperately needed. Yes, sometimes children became available for adoption. Yes, the adoption would be paid for by the state. Yes, sometimes newborns needed foster homes. I sat and thought about it. I did some more research. I joined a few message boards. And I talked about it with Sam. I became convinced that foster parenting was our best shot at getting a baby without the massive expense and the marketing and the maneuvering of traditional adoption. I wanted a baby. Babies needed homes. And maybe one of those babies would eventually need a forever home. Foster to Adopt, they called it. I decided that I was going to be the best foster mom in the history of foster moms, if it meant that I might somehow be given a shot at moving beyond foster parenting to adoption.

I was cautioned that our odds of adopting a foster child were small. The odds of adopting a newborn through foster care were infinitesimal.

I am a betting woman. And I was willing to take those odds.

My husband is not a betting man. But to his credit, Sam was willing to give it a shot. The bottom line was that being a foster parent was a good thing to do. And in the end, there might be a huge reward: there might be a baby. And that was all we needed to hear. I registered us for the next six week training session.

The classes met at the local community center on Tuesday evenings, in a drab and vaguely depressing room with fluorescent lights and metal folding chairs. Most of us were new to the foster care system, while a few couples had been foster parents before. We learned about the reasons children are taken into protective custody, and what to expect when you bring a child into your home after they have been separated – sometimes against their will – from their family. We learned about visitation, and behavioral issues, when to call for help, what you need to provide for the child by law, and what the state was able to provide. There was always a potluck dinner at the end of class, and while I would spend hours trying to cook something nutritious, many times my crockpot sat next to a box of fried chicken from the gas station down the street and a bag of chips. I wondered if they were going to feed their foster children fried chicken from the gas station for dinner. Some people told stories about over-crowded foster homes, people becoming foster parents as a job – but because the "reimbursement" for fostering a child was so little (just about $550 a month) they had to take multiple kids to cover their expenses. I wondered how that could be – our home had to be inspected, and I knew you had to have a certain income and a specific amount of space (an actual allotment of square feet) for each child in your home. How could people take so many kids? Was the system really *that* broken?

We were about to find out. At the end of the six weeks, Sam and I were presented with a certificate, stating that we had completed the necessary coursework to be licensed by the state of Hawaii. Our home was inspected, we were interviewed and fingerprinted, and then we received the license in the mail, in an unmarked manila envelope. And that was how it all began.

We were going to be foster parents, and with a little luck we were going to adopt a foster child.

That possibility, while remote, was enough.

And then we met Faith and Sophia. And everything changed.

Chapter 5 Losing Faith

Our first placement came quickly after our license was issued. We got a call asking us if we were available to take a foster child that week, and when I answered in the affirmative there was a long pause – a pause I now know signifies that the worker is figuring out exactly how much to tell me. There is full disclosure, and then there is talking a foster parent out of taking a case. The social worker took a breath and continued.

"This case is……unique."

"Okay. How unique?" I was trying to unload the groceries from the car, and Max was scooting around my feet on a tricycle while I walked back and forth.

"Well, it's actually a mom and baby."

I stopped. I must have misunderstood. "It's a what?"

Faith was 16. She had been in foster care for a while. Her parents had their rights terminated after abusing their children for years, and in addition to the challenges with her biological family, Faith had a restraining order against her boyfriend. She had been through a lot of foster homes, and now her baby was along for the ride. They needed a safe place to live, a place where she could learn how to take care of a baby, and how to take care of herself. She also needed someone to watch the baby while she went to school.

A teenager. I was only 27 years old, and I was going to parent a teenager? This was not what I had in mind.

Of course I said yes.

We moved out of our bedroom and into the guest suite at the other end of the house, setting up a crib in the spare room next to the master bedroom we had just vacated. After school the next day, a white car with the state emblem pulled slowly into our driveway. A petite teenager with big brown eyes and dark hair pulled back in a smooth ponytail got out and came towards the door.

It was, for all the world, like a job interview - and I was the one being interviewed. Faith was meeting with several foster families to decide which one she wanted to live with and who she wanted taking care of her child while she was in school. She toured the house, looking in closets and walking through each bathroom. You could see her coolly assessing our home as though she was in the market to buy it. Was this where she really wanted to live? Did this bedroom suit her? Was there enough closet space? And what kind of food was in the pantry? I felt uncomfortable, as though I needed to sell her on our family and our home. I hadn't realized that we were only one of several families she was considering until the worker mentioned it halfway through the visit. By the time she left, I sort of hoped she would choose someone else.

But she didn't. The social worker called to notify me as if I had just won the lottery: "Faith has thought about it and decided she would like to come and live with you. She'll be there tomorrow."

Faith arrived the next day with her belongings jammed into a dozen plastic garbage bags and one beat up and slightly moldy suitcase. Also in the backseat of the social workers car: a baby girl in a car seat. Sophia.

The contents of the bags smelled mildewed and slightly sour. There were piles of baby clothes of all different sizes, scuffed shoes, purses and diaper bags. Roaches, which are common in the tropics, would skitter out of pockets and folds unexpectedly. She had so much stuff we didn't really have anywhere to put it all. The double dresser that had easily held the clothes of two people just a few days before was now filled to overflowing, and the doors of the closet couldn't contain all that was within. I was astounded. How had she managed to accumulate all of this........crap? I tried to help her sort through it all – pull out the things that were too stained or torn or dirty to wear, sifting through stacks of onesies and overalls to find the things that Sophia had already outgrown, winnowing down the countless pairs of newborn sized sneakers she really didn't need. I gave her some warm clothes from my closet since everything Faith owned seemed to be short-sleeved or sleeveless, and we lived at an elevation that got quite chilly at night.

Faith, we soon learned, had a sibling on island – she was a few years older, armed with a cellphone, and attending the community college. She didn't have a car, but the sisters tried to see each other whenever possible and spent hours on the phone. I was thrilled. To know that Faith had a biological relative that she was in contact with, a sister who seemed to be on the right path in life and could be a role model for her when her parents were so clearly not up to the task was – in my mind – a blessing. I encouraged Faith to invite her sister over to visit, volunteered to pick her sister up in town and bring her to our house whenever she wanted. I wanted to foster not only Faith and her baby, but also her relationship with her sister - someone who shared her history, and would share her future as well.

In the beginning everything went really smoothly – Max loved having a "big sister" and a "baby sister", and Faith was fascinated by Max's antics, probably realizing that in just a few years Sophia would be that age. We watched movies together at night, cooking dinner together each evening, going to the beach on the weekends. I would look around the house at the kids and toys and laundry and feel pride (and surprise) at how well it was all working out. Faith was polite to us, and an attentive mother to Sophia. She went to school all day and took care of the baby during the night, bringing her into my bedroom before catching the bus at 6:30 each morning. Occasionally we would pick up her sister and bring her to our house for visits and once for a sleepover, the two of them curled up in the double bed just as I am sure they did as children. I was glad that they were together.

I knew they had endured years of mistreatment – we never discussed the specifics but they still had limited phone contact with their mother and Faith informed me that she planned to live with her mother again when she aged out of foster care. This was when I learned that as soon as a foster child turned 18, or graduated from high school, they were expected to live independently. She would be free to return to her mother's home – with her child in tow – and I was worried that the cycle of abuse would continue. It was a sensitive subject, and so I just tried to show Faith and her sister what a happy marriage and a stable home life looked like. I wanted them to have the experience of feeling safe, and secure, and cared for. I wanted them to have something to aspire to – a home and a partner, steady employment, open lines of communication, commitment and respect.

I felt like I was making a difference and as the weeks turned to months we became a family. Or so I thought. Faith confided in me somewhat wistfully that her last foster mother had fed her kids fast food every single night. She admitted that she had trouble deciding if she wanted to live with me or another foster mother – she and her sister had to decide between "the one with the long hair, and the one with the short punk rocker hair". I was bewildered. How many children were given a selection of foster parents to choose from?

Eventually, Faith started to settle in, and the "honeymoon period" everyone had warned me about came to an abrupt end. She sullenly refused to get out of bed in the middle of the night to make bottles, preferring instead to leave a bottle sitting unrefrigerated on her bedside table for the 2am feeding. She began making and receiving late night phone calls, and eventually gave her boyfriend – despite the restraining order – our home address.

As Faith regressed, the full weight of responsibility for Faith and Sophia's care fell on my shoulders, and I was frazzled from trying to manage it all – I had very little time for Max because I was always holding a baby or negotiating with an angry, overwhelmed teenager. One night when it was determined that Sophia needed to see a doctor for what I suspected was an ear infection, we packed her diaper bag and headed out the door. At the last minute, Sam decided to drive while I stayed home and spent some time with Max. When she learned of the change in plans, Faith turned on her heel and handed the baby to me to buckle up while she headed back to her bedroom. As I secured Sophia in her carseat, Faith came sauntering out of her room in a short, tight miniskirt and a midriff bearing top. Sam raised an eyebrow and tossed me the keys. "Never mind," he said. "You take her."

I smiled half-heartedly and watched Sam and Max head back inside to play trains, while Faith – who was visibly disappointed that I was the one taking her to the clinic in my old sweatpants and milk-stained tee shirt – got in the front seat with a sour look on her face.

I had a lot of sympathy for her. She was struggling to take care of a baby and attend school and trying all the while to figure out how she was going to co-parent for the next 18 years, when the other parent was no more than a kid himself. I knew that she was acutely aware of all she was missing both by becoming a mother at 16, and by living in an isolated area on the mountain so far from town. I tried to give her some freedom, dropping her off at the mall on Saturday afternoons with a $20, letting her spend hours with her sister and her friends, pushing the stroller through the stores and grabbing lunch at the food court. I remembered what it was like to be a teenager. I wanted her to have some semblance of a normal life.

One weekend before Thanksgiving, I offered to watch the baby overnight so that she could spend a night in the dorm with her sister. I thought it might inspire her to see what college was really like, to be in the dorm surrounded by kids her own age who were continuing their education. I hoped the experience would encourage her to keep going, to stay in school, to dream big and work hard. And I thought she deserved a night off.

My phone rang at 7am the next morning, and a woman on the other end of the line said "Faith just walked out of my bathroom in my son's t-shirt and nothing else. I don't want him getting in trouble. She shouldn't be here."

I stared at the caller ID and realized that her "son" was the boyfriend. The father of the baby I was holding. The boy who was, apparently, violating the terms of his restraining order. "Thank you for letting me know." I hung up the phone and realized afterwards that I hadn't asked for the address.

I went to my filing cabinet and found the paperwork from our licensing classes. There was an emergency hotline number, and with shaking hands, I called it.

The woman who answered the phone got straight to the point. "Do you know where she is?"

"No. All I know is she is in town. Someone just called from the house where she was a few minutes ago, but it's not a landline and I am sure she is leaving now that they've been found out. She's not answering her cell, and I called her sister and she didn't know where she was either. At first she tried to pretend that Faith was asleep, I guess she was trying to cover for her. But I called her on it, and she said she didn't know where she was. She didn't spend the night at the dorm. I have the baby here. The baby is with me."

"The baby?"

"Her baby. Faith's baby. Her baby girl is here with me."

"Are you also *her* foster mother?"

"No, she's not in state custody, she's not a foster child. That's just Faith."

"So, you have her baby, but you can't get in touch with her, and you don't know where she is? What if there was an emergency with the baby? You aren't that baby's foster parent. You have to be able to get in touch with her mother."

"Well, I thought I knew where she was. She was supposed to be at the dorm and I......." I trailed off. What could I say?

The social worker sighed and said "You have to call the police. Especially with a restraining order involved. She could be in danger."

My phone call that morning set off a series of events. The police were called, Faith was reported as a runaway, and at some point that day they picked her up in town. I packed a bag for her with some clean clothes and her bath stuff, and drove it down the mountain, crying the whole way. My first case – my very first try at foster parenting - and *I had lost the kid*. This had to be some kind of record. If they fired foster parents, I was totally going to be fired.

But I wasn't. Apparently, Faith had quite a history of disappearing. When her social worker tried to talk to her, she accused us of mistreating her. She said that I was causing Sophia's ear infections, and that Sam was flirting with her. According to the social worker, Faith also had a history of making these types of claims when she wanted a transfer. And so, she got what she wanted. She was transferred to a new foster home. Sam was horrified by the allegations, and there really wasn't anything I could say to make it less offensive. Here we were trying to help, and instead we got....this?

We couldn't imagine moving Sophia to another foster home – she was happy and settled, and so her custody was turned over to me temporarily. Sam and I moved back into the master bedroom next to her nursery. And when we went to pack up all of Faith's belongings to send on to the new foster home, Sam found that Faith had more problems than either of us had realized. Following a suspicious smell and a few roaches, he discovered food rotting under the bed, and worse: used maxi pads wrapped in toilet paper in the back of a drawer. The social workers were not surprised. We were informed – belatedly – that this was a known behavior of children who had been victims of sexual abuse. This was also the first specific detail we were given about the abuse Faith had experienced during her childhood – and a piece of information that I think should have been disclosed at the outset. By the end of the week, I was beginning to have some serious concerns about my decision to take this case. Maybe this foster parenting thing was not such a great idea.

Chapter 6 Sophia, herself

"This worked out exactly like you planned. You always wanted to keep her for yourself" Faith hissed into the phone. "Now you have the baby you wanted so badly."

I sighed and leaned against the wall in the kitchen, resting my head on the side of the phone that hung there, twisting the phone cord between my fingers. The answering machine blinked with messages that I didn't have the energy to listen to. I stared at the new box of ovulation predictors on the counter. This was an unmitigated disaster.

Once we had called the police, and they had located Faith, I was contacted by a social worker to ask if I wanted them to bring her back to my home. I answered as honestly as I could: I didn't think I was prepared to parent a teenager. I didn't want to have her living in our house on lockdown, but I realized now that there were no guarantees – every time she left the house I didn't really have any control over where she went, what she did, or whether she would return. I knew that as a parent that was part of the deal. And I wasn't ready for it. I would be a nervous wreck. And what if she got pregnant again, or continued to sneak away to her ex-boyfriend's house in violation of the restraining order?

It was the week of Thanksgiving. I just wanted to sit down and have a family dinner – and the family was a complete mess. I was a complete mess. This was not what I had in mind when I read that ad about the foster program last summer. All I had to show for my effort was a sullen teenager and a baby in limbo.

As a result of my honest self-assessment and Faith's bizarre accusations, the social worker had agreed to move Faith to a new home - the one that she had been considering when she first moved in with us. Sophia stayed with me while the state figured out the details. And Faith was *livid*. Meanwhile, my role in all of this was not over – far from it. I had to meet with an investigator, talk to another social worker, and still try to get through the holiday season with my sanity intact. It was a nightmare, and Faith was living the same one. I tried to keep that in mind.

"Faith, Sophia is your baby. I don't want your baby – I want a baby of my own."

She was silent on the other end of the line. I leaned forward and pushed myself to standing. I had a load of laundry to get in the dryer, and this phone call was freaking me out.

Usually when foster parents have custody of a child, the biological parents don't have the foster home's phone number - and they certainly don't call you at all hours to tell you what a horrible person you are for taking their kid away. This was a special circumstance. What had the worker called it? Unique?

Yeah, this was unique all right.

"I gotta go." She muttered into the phone. I could hear kids behind her laughing and shouting. I couldn't tell if she was inside or sitting out on a picnic table under one of the trees in the school yard. I hoped that she was wearing the sweatshirt I had packed, but it wasn't something I was going to ask her. I didn't ask her *any* questions – I just listened, and let her say all of the horrible things she needed to say. I knew it wasn't just me that she was angry at - she was angry at the world. But my number was the one she called when she needed to yell at someone. I figured this was what parenting a teenager was like. I had memories of being this angry, and taking it out on my mother. The only difference was, I didn't have a cellphone when I was 16. It's easier to say hateful things over the phone, than to someone's face. And I didn't have a baby being raised by a stranger against my wishes.

This was awful. I felt totally responsible. If I had kept her home that night, forbidden her to sleep over, not reported her missing to CPS…….every way I looked at it, this was my fault. I didn't blame her for being angry at me – I was angry at myself. It felt as though I had done more harm than good, and I couldn't fix it.

"Okay. Sophia will see you in a few days." I reminded her. "The transport worker said she would pick her up at 2pm."

"Yeah. Whatever."

-click-

I turned and put the receiver back in the cradle. I heard Sophia stirring in the other room, and I went to peek in and check on her. We were settled back into our bedroom, and I had filled at least a half dozen garbage bags with the clothes and toys and accessories and gear that Faith had brought with her, and added the things we had bought for her. The social worker had picked it all up the day Faith moved into her latest foster home. After all of the drawers and the closet and the floor under the bed were cleared out, we pulled out all of the furniture, and bombed the room for roaches since so many of them had arrived when she moved in. Until recently, the room had smelled ever-so-faintly of chemicals, a reminder of just how bad things had been.

I picked Sophia up out of her crib and carried her into my bedroom, laying her down on the bed and tickling her cheeks while she grinned and cooed at me. Max wandered in and climbed up on the bed next to her, patting the silky black waves that had recently grown long enough to curl over Sophia's ears.

We sat there for a while, Max patting Sophia's head absent-mindedly while he watched Sesame Street. I folded laundry and contemplated changing our phone numbers. I really didn't want to, but these phone calls were starting to wear on me. I decided to hold off another few weeks. I hoped that maybe things would improve. But when Sophia came back from her visit with Faith a few days later, she was fussing in her carseat as the worker passed her to me in the driveway. Her eyes looked strange, sort of glassy and distant. I set the carseat down on the dining room floor and unbuckled her, realizing as soon as I rested her on my shoulder that she was very, very hot. I went and got the thermometer.

As I tried to hold the thin case steady in her ear, Sophia twisted and turned and cried – making it impossible to get a reading. I tried to soothe her, but she became more upset with each passing moment. Finally she quieted and I could keep the thermometer in place. When it beeped twice and I checked the screen, my heart stopped. "103F" the screen said. I pressed "clear" and put it in the other ear. "102.7F" the screen said.

"Oh *man*." I muttered under my breath as I exhaled. "Max, buddy" I said apologetically "we need to take the baby to the doctor." I dialed the clinic number on my cellphone as I put Sophia back in her carseat. She instantly began crying again. I grabbed the bottle of Tylenol off the counter and gave her a dose before I shoved open the front door and climbed into the back of the van to strap her in. Max clambered in after me clutching a bag of goldfish and a juicebox, settling down into his carseat and waiting patiently for his turn to buckle up. He was always up for a car ride in the van.

I hated that van. It was hideous, first of all. I hate minivans in general, and this one was particularly awful. Maroon, with gold accents – Sam and I called it the pimpmobile. But when Faith and Sophia moved in, we needed to get a bigger car. I couldn't fit two carseats and a teenager in the back of my Civic no matter how many different ways I tried. So we had gone to the used car lot – all of us together - and brought home this monstrosity of a minivan. Faith and Max had begged us to buy this particularly hideous model because it had a television. The two of them would sit silently in the back row staring at the screen that was suspended from the ceiling, watching movies whenever we drove anywhere. Most of the time, it made me nuts.

Today I had a movie playing before I buckled my seatbelt.

It was dinner time, and now I had a 40 minute drive to the doctor's office, a wait of god knows how long in the clinic, and then a drive back home. If they wanted to watch The Muppet Show then darnit, they were going to watch the Muppet Show. "I WANT THOMAS!" Max yelled from the back row of seats.

I stood corrected: If they wanted Thomas the Tank Engine, well that was okay too.

Sophia fell asleep a few minutes into the ride, and as I drove down the highway I didn't spend a moment enjoying the gorgeous view or the cool breeze. All I could think about was the number flashing on the thermometer screen, and how no one else – not her mother, or her foster mother, or the parenting educator that had been with them supervising the visit – no one had noticed that she was ill. How could NO ONE have noticed that she felt warm? That her back was scorching hot to the touch, her skin dry and taut and her eyes unfocused? I fumed as I drove carefully through the 5 o'clock traffic. At the pediatrician's office, they whisked us in the back and began checking her vitals, taking her temperature (which was going down in response to the Tylenol) monitoring her heart rate, weighing her, all the while peppering me with questions:

When had I noticed the fever? Had she been sleeping well? Any unusual fussiness? Because her fever was still high, the pediatrician saw us right away, which was a relief. I held Sophia in one arm, and balanced Max on my other knee. I was worried that Max might get sick but there was no point in separating them now. Besides, there were probably more germs in the exam room than anything he could catch from Sophia.

"Another ear infection" the doctor pronounced after a quick assessment. "She has a double ear infection. I'm pretty sure that is the problem, everything else looks okay. And how do YOU feel?" she asked, turning to Max, who was scribbling away on the back of my checkbook. "Good." He said cheerfully, his eyes never leaving his masterpiece.

"I'm going to check him anyway" the doctor said to me under her breath. "Don't want you to have to make another trip later on." I smiled weakly, and tried to remember a few months ago, when I had thought this was going to be easy.

Max was thoroughly poked and prodded, and pronounced in excellent health. We headed home with a paper bag full of antibiotics for Sophia, and another paper bag filled with a Happy Meal for Max. All I wanted to do was climb into bed and stick my head under the pillow for a few days. But there was far too much going on for that. It was a few weeks before Christmas, almost Max's birthday, and our days were a blur of projects, shopping, and standing in line at the post office to mail packages to our relatives on the mainland.

It was my first holiday as a foster parent, and I wasn't sure exactly how to handle it. My mother wanted to send gifts for Sophia, but I couldn't be sure she would still be living with me by then. We were attending holiday events and festivals every week, seeing friends for the first time in weeks or months – many of whom didn't know that we were fostering. When we went to holiday parties, people frequently assumed Sophia was our child. We were met with squeals and congratulations everywhere we turned. And each time, I thanked them politely or explained the situation, depending on how much time I had, and how well I knew them. But one thing remained constant each time I received their good wishes: I thought of Faith, who was surely heartsick about not being with her daughter.

There wasn't much I could do about it, so I just dug in and went about my day, every day, as the mother of two. Because after all, Sophia was - for all intents and purposes - my child. At least for the time being. She slept in a carrier strapped to my chest as I ran errands, she and Max took baths together giggling and splashing, and each night I would rock her to sleep. One afternoon, we stopped at a walk-in portrait studio and got holiday photos taken of Max and Sophia – photos which I resolutely stuck in every card. I didn't feel right excluding Sophia from the photo, but we got a lot of frantic phone calls from extended family and friends back in New England, wondering who this baby was, and when she had appeared. Had they missed a birth announcement? I realized that I needed to do better about keeping everyone informed – and I started composing a letter, akin to the usual holiday newsletter some families send out. Instead of the letters I was used to receiving, touting everyone's accomplishments for the year, detailing the vacations taken with accompanying photographs of people I only vaguely knew, my letter was packed full of breaking news - I outlined our move to a new home, Faith's brief time with us, and Sophia's current and future plans, which seemed to change by the week. I am sure the letter read like an after-school special, but it couldn't be helped. It was how my life was. A few people voiced concern that I liked to make things complicated – as though, by choosing to be a foster parent, I was somehow trying to cause more stress and drama for myself. A year before, I had thought fostering was going to be an easy solution to a simple problem, but I was starting to think that maybe they were on to something. Because this was a lot more drama than I had bargained for.

A few weeks later, I got a certified letter in the mail: a summons. Faith was going to court to regain custody, and I was being called to testify.

The judge was going to decide two things: would Sophia live with me, or with Faith. And, would she be in Faith's custody or in state custody. State custody meant that Faith would have more resources – financial and otherwise – but it also meant more oversight both of her parenting, and of Sophia's development. I didn't know if that was necessarily a bad thing. But no matter whether Sophia was in the custody of the state or her mother, I wanted them to be together in the same foster home again. Neither of them deserved to be living apart.

I emptied the drawers of her dresser the night before the court date, carefully folding all of the clothes I had bought her, and the few things I had salvaged from the stacks of moldy baby clothes all of those months ago when she had first moved in with Faith. I packed everything up, and then went to the pantry and pulled out the baby food, formula and bottles. Faith was going to need all of it, and I would not.

I refused to let myself believe that Sophia would stay with us after court – she needed to be with her mother. And her mother needed to be with her. I was sure that the state would do the right thing and reunite them – in whatever form that would take legally.

As I sat outside the courtroom, I felt like I might throw up. I didn't want to see Faith, I didn't want to tell the story, or discuss whether or not I thought she was capable of parenting. I had no interest in any part of this. I wanted someone to wrap it all up in a shiny bow and make it better -preferably without my assistance.

After speaking with a bailiff and getting assurances that they wouldn't need me for a while, I went into the ladies room. When I came out of the stall, Faith was standing there washing her hands and watching me in the mirror. If looks could kill, hers had "homicide" written all over it. In retrospect, I was probably just panicking – but in the moment, I was horrified.

I became a foster parent to adopt a child, and instead of going to family court to sign adoption papers, I was here to testify so that I could give someone back their baby. And now, clearly, I was going to die in the courthouse ladies room. Fantastic.

"Hi there." I plastered a weak smile on my face and approached the sinks cautiously.

Faith glared at me.

"Listen," I began with a deep breath. "I am here to tell them I think Sophia should be with you. I have never thought any differently."

Silence.

"They might not even need me to testify," I continued. "I gave a statement already. They know how I feel."

Silence.

"So, I hope everything works out today." I wanted to give her a hug, but I still thought she might smack me. I backed towards the door before hustling back to the safety of my bench in full view of the bailiff.

It turns out I didn't need to testify – they came to an agreement in the courtroom and the social worker came out and asked me to go get

Sophia ready – she was being picked up in a hour and going to live with Faith. "She's already packed." I said with relief. "I just need a few minutes to get her toys together."

I headed straight for the house, pausing to call Sam and let him know what was going on. When I walked in the door he had moved all of the baby gear outside to the driveway. I sat in the middle of the living room and dismantled the exersaucer, and tried not to cry.

The worker arrived to pick Sophia up, and we spent a while loading the car – over the past few months we had managed to accumulate every baby item you could imagine, and it took some effort to fit it all in the back of the sedan. But in the end, it was just the baby left to be put in the back seat, and I hesitated.

When I walked over to pick her up, she looked up at me with big brown eyes, smiling and lifting her arms in anticipation of a cuddle. I grinned through my tears and rested my face on the top of her head, burying my nose in her hair. Sam watched from the kitchen. The social worker stood outside of our open front door, leaning against her car parked in the driveway with the door ajar and the chime ringing over and over again. I wanted to ask her for a minute, but in my heart I knew it would be easier to just say a quick goodbye. Max wandered over and I bent down to squeeze his shoulder – Sophia leaned towards him and grabbed his curls. "OW!" Max hollered, startling all of us. I carefully unwound the baby's fingers from his ringlets, and walked outside. Max was used to the baby leaving for visits, and it took him a minute to realize that all of the baby's toys were going with her this time. He began to cry. I handed Sophia to the worker. And then I turned and reached for Max. He needed his mother, just as much as Sophia did.

Chapter 7 The Clothes on His Back

After the months we spent with Faith and Sophia, the next placement seemed like a whirlwind. It had taken me a while to recover from the trauma of seeing a child I had cared for - no matter how briefly - walking into a courtroom, shooting me angry looks en route to asking the judge to be given custody of her child. It felt like some sort of crazy twilight zone. Was this what parenting was? Would I see my own little golden haired toddler in a courtroom one day, begging a judge for leniency while I paced the hallway outside?

Maybe it was better to just take children short-term. No risk of getting attached and then having to say goodbye. It would be easier, and safer. Less risk, and less emotional investment. But it probably wouldn't be an issue for a while, anyway: the social workers had told me from the beginning that babies were few and far between. So I pulled myself together and got a job – I worked as a concierge of sorts, and my client base was far-reaching. Most lived on the mainland, and were planning trips to Hawaii and needed advice about where to stay and what to do while they were here. I love living in Hawaii, and I love giving advice and making suggestions – the job was a perfect fit. It kept me busy – and distracted. It also allowed me to be home with Max several mornings a week, to assuage the mommy guilt. I figured it would be a while before I got another call from CPS, and I just put it out of my mind.

Which is why, when my phone rang as we were leaving story time at the local library a few weeks later, I wasn't expecting to see *"Hawaii State Gov"* flash on the screen.

I answered with a cautious "Hello?"

The person on the other end was speaking quickly. There were not a lot of details. An infant. Parents in police custody. Could I take him while they figured out where the next of kin were?

Of course I said yes. I had one question: Do I have time to grab formula and diapers?

The worker paused and covered the phone to ask someone nearby what the time frame was. It was going to be tight - they were on their way. The worker would be at my house in 45 minutes.

I ran through Foodland throwing a can of formula, a few bottles, and a bottle brush in the cart. I stopped in front of the diapers and had a moment of panic. What size? I scanned the packages, deciding on a size 3. I could always roll them down to make them smaller, right? Max was sitting in the cart, telling everyone who walked by that we were getting a baby. People looked perplexed. I could relate.

I had barely washed the bottles when a familiar white car with the state emblem on the door rolled up. The worker climbed out, came around the back and bent over into the backseat. She emerged holding a blonde infant wearing only a diaper, with a small flannel receiving blanket clutched to his chest. He was squalling, twisting in the workers arms.

Thomas had arrived hungry.

We went through the formalities: while Max lay on the floor entertaining the baby, I signed the paperwork making me Thomas' custodian. I was told his name and date of birth, and then the worker headed for the door.

I jumped up.

"Wait. That's it? Does he have any clothes? Did you take him to get checked out by a doctor when you took him from his parents? What if he's hurt, or sick? How much does he weigh? Do you know what brand of formula he drinks? Does he have any allergies? Is he teething? Has he started solid food?"

"I don't know anything more than what is on that form. They didn't give me any personal belongings. He hasn't seen a doctor, but his worker should know more tomorrow. They'll give you a call."

She closed the door behind her, and was gone.

Max looked up from the floor, where Thomas was chewing on his fingers and staring at the ceiling fan. "Mama, I think he has a poop." After changing his diaper and tracking down a shirt that I could get snapped around him (the first one I had pulled out of the attic was too small), he was clearly very hungry. I made a bottle and just hoped that he wasn't allergic to dairy. It was the best I could do.

Allergic or not, he refused to eat it, wincing and batting his hands around, turning his head, thrusting his tongue out and sending formula flying. I had no idea what to do. He was obviously hungry. He cried and cried and cried. After about an hour, I put him in our spare infant carseat, grabbed a baby sling from the closet, and we drove back to the store, Thomas crying the whole way. Maybe he needed a different brand or something? I was at a loss.

I stood in the aisle with Thomas in the sling, frantically chewing on the fabric and twisting with what I assumed was hunger and frustration. Max was once again in the cart, introducing everyone who walked by to the baby. "We just got him today" he proclaimed proudly. The women all stopped to peek and coo at him, while asking Max pointed questions, hoping to get the details out of this enthusiastic and chatty three year old. I scanned the brands and decided to get a few different small cans, adding in my head trying to figure out if I could afford three or four. Four would be better – maybe he needed soy.

This stuff was crazy expensive. I ended up buying three kinds of powdered formula, two small cans of liquid formula, four types of nipples, a different style of bottle for him to try, and before we went to the checkout I grabbed a bottle of wine for *me* to try. It looked like this was going to be a very long day.

Several hours later, I had convinced him to eat something – he had finally accepted a formula/nipple combination after much trial and error. The kitchen counter was covered with cakes of powdered formula, sticky puddles of ready-made formula, and three bottles that had been discarded after he had refused to touch them. I was on my second glass of wine, and it wasn't even 4pm. Thomas and I were both exhausted and sweaty, covered in milk, and ready to cry. Max had been eating a Costco sized box of goldfish crackers for the past two hours, watching Thomas the Tank Engine videos and occasionally wandering over to pat the baby gently on the head and tell him that he was named after a train.

It went on like that for…I don't know. Maybe two days? Could have been longer – it certainly felt like an eternity. We did the same dance at every feeding. He would wake up screaming with hunger, I would go through three or four bottles trying to convince him to eat something, and eventually he would give in – probably because he was too hungry to care anymore. I called the social workers and asked them if someone could PLEASE ask his mother what the trick was. I was out of options. They were not really any help: not only did they not get any information from the mother, but they seemed totally ignorant about the needs of an infant in general.

I decided to take him down to the doctor, to be sure he wasn't sick. A social worker planned to meet me at the appointment so that she could be "in the loop". She wasn't sure that this doctor's appointment was necessary, but I figured it couldn't hurt. He was supposed to be seen by a doctor before he had been brought to my home to begin with – yet another example of protocol completely abandoned in the face of real-life scenarios that didn't fit the mold. After days and days of crying, I was starting to wonder - maybe he had an ear infection? The pediatrician examined him thoroughly and while his ears were clear, she thought that he might be teething. The doctor recommended that I give him Tylenol and see if it helped. As she gave me my instructions and went over the dosage, the social worker was busily taking notes. Suddenly, she stopped scribbling and looked up. "Wait. Is this Tylenol in *liquid* form?"

The doctor and I both stopped talking and turned to look at her, our mouths agape. I had Thomas on my shoulder, patting his back gently as he sucked on the burp cloth. It took all of my self-restraint to not say "No, we're going to get the caplets, actually."

The pediatrician, however, was alarmed. "Yes, of course it would be in liquid form. He is an *infant.* He would be taking infant Tylenol. *Which is liquid.*" She shook her head as she turned back to me and shot me a look that said "Who *is* this joker?" I raised an eyebrow and we resumed our conversation about different ways I could try to make Thomas more comfortable.

The Tylenol didn't make any difference at all, so I turned my focus back to his feedings. We eventually bought nine different types of formula, offering him each one, sometimes several different types during a single feeding. And each time he would rear back and send milk spraying into my face as though I was trying to poison him. One morning I was standing in the formula aisle yet again, trying to figure out which brand I hadn't already purchased and tried to feed him, when a braless, earthy mama sidled up to me. "Breast is best!" she said cheerfully. I scowled at her. "No, really. This stuff is all crap." She said, waving at the shelf in front of us as though she was confiding in me. "Tastes terrible. Your own milk is the best thing you could give that baby." She leaned over and cooed at poor Thomas, who was staring vacantly into space, having given up on me ages ago. "And think of all that money you would save if you breastfed him!"

"We just got him last week!" Max explained helpfully from the back of the carriage.

"He's not my baby." was the only civil thing I could think of to say. I reached over and plucked Thomas out of the carseat, holding him close. We both looked at her menacingly: Thomas with hunger, me with rage. I had come to the end of my rope, and was clinging to the very frayed edges of my sanity. If she said one more word, there was going to be a problem.

She looked taken aback, perhaps sensing that we were not her target audience, and she edged away muttering to herself, grabbing a package of "natural" diapers as she walked down the aisle. "You're killing the planet with those things!" I shouted after her. "Cloth is a much more responsible choice!" She shot me a look over her shoulder and Thomas and I both grinned. "Say Bye Bye Thomas" I cooed. And then I turned back to the formula.

But my mind was reeling. I stopped looking at the cans on the shelf, and thought about what she had said. Yes, it was insensitive......yet I wondered if I had ever thought – or even (god forbid) *said* – those things myself? Had I ever made a comment about the superiority of breastfeeding to someone who chose not to breastfeed? It sounded hauntingly familiar. I was thoroughly indoctrinated in the benefits of breast milk – after all, they were listed ad nauseum in brochures and books and on posters in my pediatrician's office. I understood where this woman was coming from, and part of me agreed with her. I had always been an ardent proponent of breastfeeding - probably because it had been pretty easy for me. But I suddenly realized that I made a great assumption when I thought that almost everyone using formula did so without much consideration. In my previous life, I had believed that only a few people truly couldn't breastfeed, and that choosing formula was somehow a lesser choice. Never mind that it was certainly none of anyone's business but the mother herself.

In just a few months of mothering other women's children I had learned a lot, but I hadn't realized how much my parenting style – and my approach to life in general - had changed until this very moment: I had been such a know it all in the beginning. Every answer was found in a book and every product was organic, or the newest and latest model. There was the right way (my way) and the wrong way (everyone else's way) to do everything. Standing in that grocery aisle, I had a moment of revelation. I had been judgmental of others and hard on myself – and it was exhausting to be so uptight. In caring for Sophia and now Thomas, I was realizing that there were a lot of ways to parent, and they all seemed to work just fine. Mothers didn't need to co-sleep, breastfeed, cloth diaper, and strap the baby to their chest 24-7, to love and care for a child, and for the child to feel safe and be healthy. In retrospect, my attitude had been pompous.

And I was ashamed. I don't know if it was the fatigue, or the innocent baby I was trying my best to care for, but I had suddenly grown up - standing there in Foodland, I felt for the first time that I had some perspective.

That afternoon, after yet another trial and error process that left us both exhausted, Thomas had cried himself to sleep. I took the opportunity to climb into the shower for a few minutes of peace and quiet. Just a few. As I rinsed the shampoo from my hair I heard a cry from down the hall. I sighed, turned off the water and reluctantly wrapped a towel around myself, padding down the hallway leaving wet footprints behind me.

"Oh honey, it's okay." I tried to comfort him, leaning over the crib and pulling him towards me. My towel came untucked and slid down towards my waist as I put him on my shoulder, and Thomas lunged. I thought I was going to drop him, but he had no intention of letting go. He grabbed my right breast with both fists and jammed my nipple in his mouth, sucking frantically.

Oh Thomas.

I sank down into the rocking chair next to his crib, trying frantically to separate him. Max had only been weaned for a year or two, and I felt my chest lurch, the familiar sensation causing a reaction in my body that I had no way to control. Poor Thomas was not going to let go. I had my finger in the corner of his mouth and I was trying to break the seal, without breaking his heart. His eyes were closed tight, and his fists reflexively grasped and released my skin like he was trying to milk me.

"Thomas, sweetheart, that isn't going to work." I pleaded with him, trying desperately to get my finger between me and his mouth. He was so hungry, and I knew now why he reacted to a bottle like it was a foreign object.

Because it was.

I managed, eventually, to pry him off me. My chest was bruised and red from his grasp, and my nipple felt raw. I grabbed the bottle that had been rejected and left on the nightstand 10 minutes before, and I held him close to my chest, almost as though he was breastfeeding, and hoped for the best. He may have been distracted or confused, but whatever the reason, he ate that bottle, and another one. And then he fell into a deep sleep. I called the social worker in tears. "Did you know he was breastfed? Can his mother feed him, at least?"

No, she couldn't. But the worker did have news: the family had been located, relatives on the mainland. A social worker would be bringing him to them in a few days. I sat back, heartbroken for this little boy and his mother. No wonder he was inconsolable. He had been separated from his mother and his food source in one fell swoop. And then something clicked in my head.

Wait.

I knew that town – the one my social worker had just mentioned, the one on the mainland. That name was familiar. Why was it…….I ran to my file cabinet and pulled open the bottom drawer, shuffling through the files until I found the right one. This couple had just booked their honeymoon with me. They were from this town……and he was a social worker.

With trembling hands I made the call.

Without disclosing any identifying information, so as to adhere to the privacy policy, I explained that I had custody of a baby on Maui. I waited a beat. He was being returned to his family in a few days, and did this man possibl-

He interrupted me, and speaking very carefully he reassured me that he knew exactly what I was talking about. He told me that a woman he knew was traveling to Maui on a case, and gave me her first name, and assurances that he would keep a special eye on Thomas' case. "Small world." he said as we hung up.

"Yes. It sure is." I agreed.

So I sat down and wrote a letter. I explained that Thomas would only drink from these particular bottles, that he only liked this specific formula. That he had been breastfed. That he was grieving. And then I packed a diaper bag carefully for his flight.

Plenty of bottles and formula.

A few changes of clothes.

Diapers and wipes.

And on top, I tucked his small flannel blanket. The only thing he had come with.

Chapter 8 For Keeps

By the time we finished our first year of foster parenting, I have to admit: I was feeling pretty defeated. It's not that I had expected to adopt a child in a year – in fact, I was pretty clear that it might never happen. But I hadn't realized how difficult it would be to care for children temporarily – and when I thought about the things that I found difficult about it, I felt selfish and embarrassed. It wasn't the emotions of giving the children back to their biological families; I felt prepared for that part, and while it could be sad, I was very matter of fact about it. I looked at foster parenting as a job – almost like a nanny, because I had experience nannying, and I was able to put a label on what was expected of me. I was not parent, I was just the caretaker.

What I found truly difficult to come to terms with, to balance in my head, was the level of commitment required to foster parent. Yes, it was temporary. Yes, the babies could come and go with a moment's notice. But rather than feeling in control of the situation, I felt like a marionette on a string. Someone else was calling the shots – and I didn't like the lack of control. All I had to do was look at the hideous minivan in my driveway and realize that my life had changed completely, and was – in a way – out of my hands. When we had enrolled in the foster parenting program, I was so focused on foster-to-adopt, and "the one call" that we would be waiting for, I hadn't thought too much about the interim – the possibility of being assigned other cases in the meantime, and how that was going to work. The reality of that – of having to drop everything with 45 minutes' notice and take a leave of absence from work to care for a baby, having to keep baby gear stacked in closets and piled on the guest room bed, and that van I was stuck driving around...... it felt like our whole life revolved around whether we might – or might not – get a call from CPS. And when we *did* have custody of a foster child, our schedule had to accommodate their very busy schedule of therapy, parent visits, doctor's appointments, meetings with the guardian, and various commitments we had to fulfill on their behalf. Something we hadn't considered at all before signing up was that we weren't able to go on vacation while we were fostering, or visit our family on the mainland, unless we found someone to provide respite care for the foster child. We couldn't take the kids in our custody off island without the permission of the biological families, who were loath to give up a visitation – which ruled out even a quick weekend away. And I was afraid that in taking a short-term placement, they wouldn't call us with a potential adoption because we were already caring for a foster child. We had only had a few placements so far, and I was left feeling confused, frustrated, and unsure that foster care or even adoption was the right choice for us. It hadn't been hard to give the babies back – it had been so easy, in fact, that I worried even more about being able to bond with an adopted child. I was concerned that the way I felt about caring for foster kids is how I would feel about raising a child we adopted. Would I always be so detached?

As a foster parent, I felt like a babysitter instead of a mother.

Not that I had anything to worry about: not a single peep had come from CPS about a child that was available for adoption – and I had asked numerous times. I knew that it was unusual to adopt an infant through foster care, so it's not that I was surprised or disappointed that it hadn't happened….I was just not sure if foster-to-adopt was what we really wanted after all. However, the one thing I did not have any question about was expanding our family. I was determined to have another child, and as our son approached his 4th birthday I realized that if I wanted to have kids that were even vaguely close in age, I had better step up my efforts, because ovulation predictors weren't miracle workers. I had a uterus, and I was about to turn 30. Didn't my chances of getting pregnant after thirty drop precipitously from their already low levels? Adoption was supposed to be our "plan B" – and "plan A' was at a standstill. I felt something like a mid-life crisis coming on.

So I did the only reasonable thing I could do at a time like this: I bought a convertible.

I also increased my hours at work and hired a nanny – a young single mom moved into our guest room with her little girl. Life shifted into a very predictable schedule. As we began to feel more settled, I called my ob/gyn and made an appointment. For the past year I had been charting temperatures, taking a fairly nasty bunch of herbs and tinctures, and checking cervical mucus – something that was just beyond disgusting. I had peed on more sticks – ovulation predictors and pregnancy tests – than any of my friends would ever have to. I had used every brand and style, with cups, droppers, pink x's and blue lines. And every one of them was negative. It was time to start talking about "medical intervention". In other words: fertility drugs.

Dr. Dee walked in the room smiling, bright and cheerful as always. She has the greatest bedside manner - even in the most difficult times she is smiling and upbeat, gentle and relaxed. "Hey there, how are you? What's going on?"

I lay back on the crinkling white paper. "I'm not pregnant." I stated flatly. "Not pregnant. At all. Nothing. Lots of sex, no baby."

"I see. Well, okay then, let's try something different." She grinned at me. "Glad you're having fun trying, though!"

I smiled weakly. "Not as much fun as we had in the beginning, that's for sure."

"Yeah, after a while it can get old. Well, listen, we'll start up the Follistim and see what happens."

"Okay, thanks." I sat staring at my knees under the blue paper drape, trying not to cry. I was so frustrated. And tired of having something that was supposed to be so damn easy be so incredibly difficult - and expensive. I went downstairs to pick up the vials of medications at the pharmacy and tried not to pass out as I handed them my credit card. The fertility treatments would be partially covered by our insurance - with limitations. I was willing to continue down this path until we reached the end of the line: physically, emotionally or financially. And if I was being realistic, I had to accept that these treatments – covered or not – might not work. All evidence showed that there were no eggs in this henhouse. I hated to think that I was never going to have another biological child. I was 29 years old, and it seemed too soon to be giving up on my body. Foster parenting was one path to having a second child – these fertility drugs would increase my chances. I could play all of my cards. Cover all the bases. Or could I?

We started the injections a week later. I was still completely unable to give myself a shot, so Sam took on that responsibility again. He was less than thrilled but considering that I definitely had the worse end of the deal, he didn't complain. The injections were traumatic - we were both very reluctant. We would have made terrible heroin addicts. "Okay, hold still" he said each time, trying to steady his hand. "Are you ready? Should I count to three?"

"WOULD YOU JUST DO IT ALREADY?" I would spit through a clenched jaw, holding on to the side of the kitchen counter to steady myself as he grabbed the cap of the needle between his teeth and pulled it off the syringe, spitting the skinny piece of plastic into the sink as he pinched a few inches of flesh between his fingers. He tried to do it in a different spot each time, so that I didn't end up with a huge black and blue mark – but it didn't make much difference. I bruised just the same. Once again, my abdomen and thighs became marked with purple smudges and needle tracks that people would notice on the beach and look at with concern.

Each month, riddled with enormous, dark bruising, bloated and anxious, the tests would come up negative. Not pregnant. Still not pregnant. Definitely not pregnant. I wasn't ovulating regularly, if at all.

But I held onto the odds – I believed that each month increased our chances of conceiving. By the third month of drugs, I was starting to get desperate. "It works 33% of the time." I said to Sam. "So the 4th cycle will be the winner." He looked dubious, but I needed to hang onto something and I had never been good at math. It was easy to tell myself each cycle that THIS would be the one. In the meantime, I still had a wad of tampons in my purse – I was hopeful, not delusional.

And then one day my phone rang at work. It was Theresa, the woman who had led our foster parenting training. I hadn't talked to her in months. Curious, I answered the phone. "Hey you!" she said brightly.

"Hey Theresa, how are you?" I shifted the phone to my shoulder and went back to highlighting a document I was working on.

"I'm good, I'm good. Listen, I just got a phone call - a very interesting phone call." She sounded….excited. Weird. This was really weird. Why was she calling me?

"Oh yeah? What's up?" I put down the highlighter and started scrolling through my inbox. My neck was getting stiff.

"Are you still in the foster to adopt program?"

"Yeah, well, I guess so," I said hesitantly "but there doesn't seem to be a lot of adopting going on." I did not want another foster placement right now. The side effects from the medications were making me tired and emotional, and I couldn't handle any more angst – I was creating enough on my own.

"I know, it can take a while. But hey, my friend Joan works at a family planning clinic, and she just called me."

"Uhm hm?" I reached for my coffee mug and scanned an email from a client.

"She has a couple that is looking for an adoptive family."

I choked. Setting my mug down on the desk, I stood up and grabbed a napkin and walked outside to mop the mess off my skirt.

Theresa continued. "So I called Sam – I had his number written down instead of yours - and I told him what was going on. He told me to call you."

"You called Sam?" I was struggling to keep up with this conversation. "About what? I'm sorry, I am confused."

"No, *I'm* sorry, I know this is a lot to process and I hate to just dump it on your over the phone. I have a friend, she works in a clinic and a couple came in and had a pregnancy test that confirmed they are expecting a baby. They want to pursue adoption, and I thought of you guys. I have a short list of people to call, and you are at the top of that list."

"Whoah."

"I know? Crazy, right? Out of nowhere."

"Whoah. I am….. whoah." I shook my head and rested my forehead against the glass door of our office suite.

"So I was wondering if you were interested? Because I am going to give Joan your name if you are interested."

"YES!" I tried not to shout. "Definitely. We are definitely interested. We are more than interested. Yes. A solid yes. Yes. Please, yes. Yes please."

She giggled. "Okay, this is exciting! They are young, they live on island, they aren't married, but they are a couple. They live together. They had a few stipulations, things they were looking for in an adoptive family."

"Like what?"

"They didn't want the baby to be an only child. They wanted parents who led a more natural lifestyle. They wanted people who were financially secure and would raise the child here on Maui. They wanted a younger couple."

"Okay, that all sounds good. I mean, we meet those criteria."

"I know you do. You were the first people I thought of. Listen, let me call Joan and give her your information."

"Okay that would be great. Theresa….thank you."

"Oh, don't thank me! This is great! So exciting!"

"Okay, wow. Call me later, okay?"

"Absolutely. Yay!"

"Yay!" I said weakly into the phone.

I hung up and called Sam who answered the phone right away.

"Hey, did Theres-"

"YES!"

"So what did you tell her?"

"What do you mean, what did I tell her? I said yes, of course, we're definitely interested."

Sam was quiet for just a beat too long.

"What?" I tried not to snap, but I was bewildered. Why wouldn't we say yes? Wasn't this the whole point? The goal? The reason for going through all the drama of the past year? So that we could adopt?

"Well," Sam said slowly "we're doing the treatments. What if they work?"

"Then we have TWO babies. Are you nuts? That's called covering all of your bases, increasing your odds, hedging your bets....HAVE YOU LOST YOUR MIND?"

He sighed. "Two babies is a lot of babies."

"I am not arguing about this. This is absolutely not up for discussion. We are saying yes. I want another child. You want another child. And if, somehow, someone miraculously chooses us to adopt their child AND I get pregnant, then we will be doubly-blessed. You know how slim the chances are of both things happening? Like, less than one percent."

He chuckled. "Well, we did it twice yesterday. I've been really working on our odds."

"SAM THIS IS NOT FUNNY."

"I know, I know. Okay. So we said yes. Yes we would consider it. It's not definite, right?"

I groaned. "You are so naïve. No, it's not definite. There are no guarantees in this life, Sam. Especially not where babies are concerned, and definitely not in adoption. Trust me on this one."

He was quiet on the other end of the line. And then he spoke carefully. "What if I don't love another baby as much as Max? What if having an adopted baby is different. We won't know until it happens. I am really nervous about this. I just.... I don't know."

A tear rolled down my cheek. "We won't know until we know. But Sam, I can't say no to this. I just can't."

"Okay. Okay. All right. Let's see what happens."

"Probably, nothing will happen."

"Right. I'm worried for nothing."

"No, not nothing. It's worth thinking about, I guess."

"You didn't need to think about it, though."

"No sweetie," I said quietly. "I didn't need to think about it."

I went back to work, sitting at my desk quietly while my head was spinning with all of the information I had just absorbed. That night, Sam and I lay on the couch facing each other, heads propped on the armrests and feet entwined. He was still worried.

"It's just that, I don't know how I will feel about a child that isn't mine. Ours. What if it feels different? What if it feels like we felt about Sophia and Thomas? I didn't feel like their parent. I didn't love them like I love Max. They weren't mine, and I never forgot it – not for a minute. I just............I don't want to make a mistake."

I took a deep breath and grabbed his hand. "I know. I can't tell you why, but I think it will be different. We'll be there right from the beginning – and the baby WILL be ours."

"Unless they change their minds."

"Right."

We sat in silence.

"That would suck." I muttered as I picked at a cuticle.

"It would. It really would. This is just.......I just don't know if we should do it. It could be a total mess."

We went to bed in silence, not angry but tired of talking about it. All of it. Tired of documenting every move and analyzing every feeling. As I fell asleep, I was thinking about getting pregnant unexpectedly, and how wonderful it would be. Just throwing out all the thermometers and tests and syringes, cancelling the appointments, and calling the doctor with the good news.

It was almost Thanksgiving.

In the next few weeks we spoke several times with Joan, the woman from the clinic, who was helping the birth parents find an adoptive family. I spent an hour or so on the phone with her, offering up all of the information I could about ourselves, our finances, our family, and asking a few questions about the details: when was the baby due? Had the mother been to see a doctor? Was everything going all right with the pregnancy? Would it be okay with her if I tried to breastfeed?

I hesitated over that last one.

To be honest, I was hesitant to ask anything at all – I didn't want to put them off in any way. I wanted to seem relaxed, easy-going, loving -

not intense and desperate. But it was hard to hide. And the breastfeeding thing? That was important to me. Now that I had used bottles for an extended period of time, I knew that formula was expensive. Breastfeeding had come so easily for me – it seemed like the one part of being a mother that felt natural. And I thought it might help with my worries about bonding.

Joan called back with some follow-up questions from the birth parents, asking about our plans for the future, how we would support our children, whether we were planning to stay in Hawaii, whether we owned our house. They were asking all of the right questions: they wanted to be sure we were stable, and would provide a good home. I was grateful for that – they seemed clear-headed and reasonable. I couldn't imagine being in their position, but they appeared to be very at peace with their decision. I wasn't sure whether their thoroughness was a sign that they were still debating whether to keep the child, or if they were confident in their plan to go forward with adoption. I tried to relax. I focused on Max's birthday that was coming up in a few weeks, and Christmas a week later. We stopped getting calls from Joan. I wondered if they had chosen a different family.

At the beginning of the year, we went to spend the night at a resort near our home as a belated family Christmas gift: 24 hours of waterslide fun. As we walked through the lobby, my cellphone rang. "Hello?" I was walking up to the front desk, pulling out my ID and credit card, and I was distracted.

"It's Theresa. They've chosen you as the adoptive parents!"

"WHAT?" My purse fell upside down onto the floor. Max giggled and chased a lipstick across the lobby.

"They chose YOU. The baby is due on April 9th."

Sam was staring at me, and whispering "What's up? Is everything okay?"

I covered the phone. "They chose us!" I turned to the front desk clerk standing in front of me. "They chose us! We're adopting a baby!"

"Um, congratulations?" she looked uncomfortable. Sam had followed Max off across the lobby and they were standing in front of a bird cage admiring an enormous blue macaw.

"Listen," Theresa said "I've got to go, we'll talk more later, but I just wanted you to know they had decided."

"Oh, thank you. Thank you so much. I just……. Thank you."

"You are so welcome!" she said cheerfully. "Best phone call I have made in a long time!"

All we could do now was sit, and wait.

I refused to buy anything for the baby – I didn't want to jinx it. We had enough baby stuff to get along when the baby arrived without buying anything. I refused to even get diapers. We hired a lawyer who drew up the papers and met with the birth parents. They had decided that they wanted a completely closed adoption, and chose to remain anonymous. I was actually okay with that – preferred it, to be honest. One of my biggest concerns about adopting was having to maintain a relationship with the biological parents – it would be too much like foster parenting. Sam and I still both had a lot of concerns about bonding with the baby, and whether adoption would feel like fostering. To reassure ourselves, we spoke with adoptive parents and adult adopted children, and watched adoptive families interact. All that we saw and heard told us that being adopting would be different than our foster experiences, but we still had that worry in the back of our minds. And there were still so many unknowns: because we didn't meet the birth parents, and because in Hawaii caucasians are the minority, we assumed that the baby would be a different race – perhaps Asian, or Hawaiian. And there hadn't been an ultrasound as far as we knew, so we didn't know the sex of the baby either. It was all cloaked in mystery. Another concern was that the birth parents lived in a rural area several hours from the hospital. There was always the chance the baby would be born at home, or that there could be complications. And the lawyer told us that while the birth parents had filled out some preliminary paperwork, nothing could be filed until the child was actually born. There really was no way to have any measure of control. It was humbling.

By the time the due date rolled around, I was a total basket case. I had my cellphone in one hand at all times. I could barely sleep. I wandered the house, peering into the nursery over and over again wondering if I should do more to get it ready. The one thing I *had* been doing was preparing to breastfeed. I hired a lactation consultant, rented an industrial grade breast pump, and started taking hormones and herbs to try to trigger lactation. I didn't know if it was working, but I refused to give up. It was the one proactive thing I could let myself do that made me feel truly maternal, like an expectant mother. But I still worried, constantly. I started having anxiety attacks. My doctor gave me a few Xanax in the hopes that I would chill out, and maybe get some sleep. "You should sleep now." she said firmly. "You won't get any sleep once the baby arrives, you know." I knew.

We went to a birthday party on Sunday, the day after the due date. I sat at the counter in a Xanax haze, the ever-present cellphone on the counter nearby. A few of the other moms leaned against the counter around me, chatting, asking me questions about the details, staring at my cellphone every time it rang. I couldn't relax. Couldn't eat. Couldn't make small talk. What if they had changed their minds? What if they had the baby at home and decided to keep it? The thoughts raced around and around my head. I tried to distract myself. And then our host found a way to keep me busy: the house we were at for the birthday party was on the market. The agent had just called to ask if she could show it to a potential buyer. We looked around at the 40 people packed in the living room and laughed. I stood up and went to clean the bathroom – it felt so good to have something – anything – to keep my mind occupied.

An hour later we were headed down the street for pizza. Friends gently teased me as I dropped my fork, stared off into space, lost track of the conversation. But in truth we were all holding our breath. The cellphone sat in the middle of the table throughout the meal, silent.

That night, I fell apart. Not knowing was killing me. My life had been out of my control for so long. I was tired of having to count on other people. I wanted to be able to have a baby like everyone else my age, instead of hoping that someone would give up theirs. It seemed like an awful thing to hope for.

"You know," Sam said gently "Max was born 10 days after his due date. You have got to get some rest. We could have another week of this."

I rolled over and groaned. "I don't think I can take it."

"Well, you don't really have a choice. You are going to make yourself crazy. Take a Tylenol PM or something. You need to sleep."

When the sun came up the next morning, I woke up from a sound sleep. "God Bless Tylenol PM." I thought as I climbed out of bed and turned on the shower.

I headed out the door at about 7:30. Sam was waiting for our nanny to get her daughter dressed, and then he was leaving too. "I'm working on the West side today," he called as I climbed in to the car. "Call me if you hear anything, I'll need a little extra time to wrap everything up."

"Okay, I'll check in later. Love you – drive safe."

I put the top down on the convertible and coasted down the hill out of our neighborhood. It was a gorgeous day.

As I crossed the street heading towards the office, my phone rang. It was too early for anyone to be calling for work, so I figured Sam was calling to talk about dinner – we had stopped planning ahead at this point, and we were just buying food each day for dinner that night. Maybe he could stop and grab some steaks on the way home…I fished the phone out of the bottom of my purse.

"Hello?"

"Congratulations! You have a daughter. She's waiting for you in the nursery."

Chapter 9 Nature vs Nurture

The next few hours were a blur of hysterical phone calls. I sat down on the sidewalk with trembling legs, and dialed Sam's number with my feet in the gutter and my files flapping in the wind. As soon as I heard his voice, I burst into tears. "We have a daughter, Sam." I was choking and sobbing and stumbling over my words.

"What? I can't hear you. Wait, I have to close my wind-"

"WE HAVE A BABY GIRL."

"Holy shit! We do? Where are you?"

"I'm at work, well, I'm in front of work. I can't drive. I can't think. Will you come here?"

"I'm on my way."

I managed to stand up and gather my things, and then made my way up two flights of stairs to the office where Mary was sitting at the reception desk. I was crying, clutching my folders to my chest, my purse flapping open, hanging off my elbow by a single strap. The wind slammed the door shut behind me and I jumped. Mary looked up and her expression of annoyance at the disturbance changed and softened as I collapsed on a chair and buried my face in my hands, shoulders heaving.

She cupped a hand over the mouthpiece of her headset. "Are you okay?"

Patricia, my manager, was rounding the corner from her office and caught sight of me crumpled by the front door. She bustled over and squatted down in front of me, putting her hands on my knees. "What's wrong, sweetheart? What happened? What's going on?"

"Let me call you back." Without waiting for an answer, Mary hung up on whoever she had been talking to and brushed past the two of us in her non-nonsense fashion, her earphones still on, and the cord swinging wildly between her knees as she headed to the back of the office.

I raised my head, my hands shaking as I wiped the tears from my cheeks. "I have a baby girl."

"A what?" Patricia looked puzzled.

"A baby girl. We have been waiting to adopt and they chose us and she was just born and they called and told me to come to the hospital because *we have a baby girl!*" The last few words came out in a sob. I took a ragged breath as she whooped and jumped up, wrapped me in an embrace and pressed my damp face to her shoulder. "Oh honey, that is so great. THAT IS FANTASTIC!"

John rounded the corner out of his cubicle at top speed, hopping on one foot to steady himself. The office busybody, his ears had perked up at the sound of excitement in the front, and he had to be the first to know what was going on so that he could immediately instant message everyone and be the trumpeter of the news – good or bad. Didn't really matter, as long as it was breaking news, he was satisfied. "What happened? What did I miss?"

Mary came racing out of the kitchen hot on his heels, with a cup of water in her outstretched hands. "Here sweetie, have a sip of water. You are as pale as a ghost." She plunked down in the chair next to me. "Now, *what* is going on? My goodness, you are shaking like a leaf. Is everything okay?"

"The baby is here! She has a baby girl!" Patricia was jubilant, and had completely forgotten that no one had any idea what she was talking about. I was still sitting, tears streaming down my face. People were starting to end phone calls and leave their cubicles to see what the commotion was about. A crowd was gathering in the foyer, people leaning up against walls and counters and doorframes, straining for the bits and pieces of information that were being passed around in a whisper. Lori was one of the lead agents, and a surrogate mom of sorts. She was one of the only people in the office that knew about our pending adoption, and she came hurrying out of her office holding her headset in one hand and shouting "What is it? What's wrong?"

"It's a girl!" Several people were cheering now, and the word was spreading through the office.

"OH HONEY! That is fantastic!" She pushed her way through the crowd and reached for me, holding my face in both of her hands and grinning through her tears.

The cellphone that had slipped to the floor rang suddenly and everyone grabbed for it. Mary answered. "Hey there Sam. Yep, she's here. We're ALL here………..She's okay……. I think she might be in shock……yes, I know……… Are you coming here? ……… No, she definitely can't drive………mmmhm………okay I'll tell her………. Okay, see you soon."

"He's on his way." She patted my shoulder as she tucked my cell back in my purse and zipped it shut.

"I have to take some time off." I turned to Patricia "I have to go. I can't work. I think…….I think I quit."

"Honey, one step at a time. Take today off. Take as much time as you need. But don't quit yet – give yourself some time to think."

"Okay. You're right. What if they change their mind?"

"Oh no. They aren't going to change their mind." She looked at me sternly. "You go get that baby, and you bring her home. And then you decide about how much time you want to take off."

I stood up unsteadily. "I'm going to change my voicemail."

"Good idea." She patted my hand and people began to disburse. The show was over.

I sat at my desk and changed my voicemail. I put my files in a briefcase and slung it over my shoulder. I checked my email, and put on an automatic responder. And suddenly I heard banging and yelling and cheering from the front. Sam came through the office like he was crossing the finish line. You could almost hear the Chariots of Fire theme song, except he looked wild eyed and vaguely panicked. "Are you ready to go?"

I grabbed my purse and shoved my chair under the desk. "Yeah. But I don't think she's going to escape. It's okay."

We walked out of the office to cheers and good wishes and hugs and pats on the back. As I climbed in the car I realized that we didn't have anything with us. No carseat, or diaper bag, or clothes. Nothing. "Oh SHIT." I looked over at him, panicked. "We can't bring her home! WE DON'T HAVE THE CARSEAT."

"Call Mari." Sam suggested as he pulled into traffic. "And tell her to bring the camera, too."

"Right. Okay.Mari." So I called our amazing babysitter, told her what was going on, and she said that she would feed the kids, pack the car, and head down to the hospital. Then I called Stacey, my roommate from Boston and Sam's cousin. It was her birthday.

"SHE WAS BORN ON MY BIRTHDAY?!" Stacey was giddy. "That is AMAZING. It's a good sign. This is awesome. I am SO EXCITED FOR YOU!!!"

"I know, it's incredible. It's totally a sign. What a great omen. I can't believe I have a daughter."

"One of each!" Sam crowed. "Hit it and quit it!"

I rolled my eyes. "You didn't hit anything, you goofball. Stace, I gotta go. I'll call you later."

I checked the clock. Our parents were still at work. We'd have to call them later. I looked over at Sam and finally relaxed and grinned. "This is INSANE."

"Yeah it is. Call the lawyer."

The birthparents had already called him. He had just returned from the hospital, and the adoption paperwork was signed. He would head back there to meet us in a few hours. "Call me when you know where they are putting you."

"Putting us?" I was confused.

"They usually keep the babies for 24 hours after birth. Not because of the adoption, just hospital policy" he explained. "They want to make . sure the baby is doing well, and answer any of your questions. No big deal."

"Oh, okay." I was relieved – this gave us some time to get a bassinet or something for her to sleep in. And it meant Mari had a little more time to get to the hospital.

We made our way up to the maternity floor and tentatively rang the bell.

"Hello?" The nurse was cheerful.

"Uh… Hi? Um, so, we are, I got a call that uh, that uh, well, that there was a baby here for me? A baby girl?" It sounded ridiculous, like I was ordering takeout or something. This whole situation was so bizarre.

"You sure do! We've been waiting for you – come on in!"

Sam grabbed my hand and squeezed, and flashed me a big grin. It was true. This was happening.

The automatic door opened slowly, and we stepped through into a hushed hallway. A door next to us swung back and a small clear bassinet came out, followed by a nurse in brightly colored scrubs. "Are you looking for us?" she said with a grin.

"Yes. Yes we are. Oh my god, is this…….."

"This is your daughter! We didn't know what you were going to name her, so we just left the card blank."

I leaned forward and my jaw dropped open. Sam stood on his toes and peeked over my shoulder.

"Um, but……. Is she……" I looked at Sam, confused. "She looks just like *Max*!" I whispered.

"Yeah, that's…….. uh, that's weird."

I looked up at the nurse. "Is she white? Are her parents white? Causasian? Oh god, I'm sorry, that sounds so terrible but….. I thought, I mean…"

The nurse looked bemused. "You haven't met the parents?"

We shook our heads, not taking our eyes off the tiny pink bundle that was wriggling around in the bassinet. Never in our wildest dreams had we expected the baby to look like our biological child. She stared up at us, her blue eyes squinted in the bright light but unblinking.

"Yes, they are both white. And she does have pretty fair skin, but it's really hard to tell at this point, she's just a few hours old." We just stood and stared.

"Listen," the nurse said kindly. "Let's get you out of the hallway. You can use this room behind the nurse's station. We can't give you a hospital room, because you aren't a patient, so you can just sit back here, okay? There's a bathroom, and a futon. Sorry, it's kind of full of stuff, but it's free!"

She pushed a door open and pulled the bassinet through behind her. We followed, not taking our eyes off the baby.

"So, this is a pretty unique situation, usually you visit with the mom-"

I interrupted. "The birth mom, right? I think….. did they leave already? Is she ours?"

The nurse grinned. "RIGHT, sorry, *birthmom*. You're the mom, aren't you! I don't know about the legalities, but they spent time with her already, and then sent her here for you. The birthmom and dad will stay in labor and delivery until they can go home."

"Okay.....can I, may I hold her?" I was clutching the curved plastic of the cart, trying to control myself.

"Oh, sorry! Yes, of course! She's yours!"

I grinned, Sam grinned, the nurse grinned. I reached in and picked up my daughter and began to rock, ever so slowly in place. Back and forth, back and forth, I stared at her, and held her tiny hand, and Sam put his arms around both of us. The nurse busied herself with her clipboard, and then interrupted our reverie.

"Do you have a name for her?"

"Lucy." We said in unison. "This is Lucy."

"Great name!" She filled out a small square of cardboard and slid it into the pocket at the head of the bassinet. "My name is: Lucy" the card said in bold letters. It had more information, and we poured over it hungrily. 7 pounds 11 ounces. 18 inches. Born at 2:35am.

I looked over and saw Sam standing there, watching me holding our new baby. It was his turn. I sighed and reluctantly handed her over. I suddenly remembered something-

"Excuse me, can you help me find someone? One of your nurses? I hired a lactation consultant, and she works on this floor, I think."

"Judy? She's off today, but I'll call her and let her know you're here. You going to breastfeed? That's great!" Her enthusiasm seemed a little forced, and so did her smile. She looked…..worried, and made a note on the chart. Was she uncomfortable with my decision? Maybe she was just concerned about having to help me figure it out so I reassured her "I breastfed my son and it was pretty easy. I've been pumping for a few weeks, and taking some medicine and some herbs, so hopefully it will work out!"

I looked over her shoulder and saw my ob-gyn Dr. Dee walking by. "HEY!" I called. She stopped and turned, her eyes widening when she saw me. "What are you doing here?" She peeked behind me and saw Sam holding the baby. "WHO IS THAT?"

"Lucy." I was beaming. "We're adopting her."

"Wow! Look at her! Oh, she is just lovely. That's great!" Dr. Dee turned to the nurse, who was still holding the chart. "So everything is fine? She's fine?" As I went to take the baby back from Sam so I could show her off, I caught the nurse shaking her head almost imperceptibly at Dr. Dee. I returned with Lucy in my arms and grinned, and Dr. Dee turned quickly back from the nurse to examine the baby I offered her. We chatted and giggled, and I chalked up the nurse's discomfort to the strange situation surrounding the custody. She couldn't disclose anything about the birth due to privacy rules, and I definitely wanted to respect the birth parents' privacy.

A few minutes later Sam's phone rang. "Mari's here" he said. "I'll go get Max and all the stuff."

He returned 15 minutes later with a camera around his neck, a diaper bag in one hand and a carseat in the other. And Max, who was grinning from ear to ear, ran ahead – racing right past the door.

"Max, they're in here!" Sam was unwinding the camera and diaper bag straps that had gotten tangled. Max bounced through the doorway and marched up to the futon where I was reclined, Lucy asleep on my chest.

"Is that my sister?" Max asked incredulously. "Can she stay with us forever?"

"Yep, you're stuck with her." Sam laughed from the corner. He was unpacking the diaper bag, searching for the supplemental breastfeeding system that had arrived in the mail the week before.

The nurse poked her head in and asked if we needed anything. Sam gave her the rundown of what was missing from the package of tubing and plastic pieces, and she returned with medical tape and scissors, and some small bottles of formula. A few minutes later Judy walked in pulling off her suit jacket, tossing it in the corner and reaching for the baby in one motion. "Sorry, I was in a meeting! How's it going? This is so exciting, I am so happy for you." She was beaming. "Okay, so let's get started!" She leaned over and pulled up my shirt, and then pulled one side of my bra down. She pinched my nipple between her thumb and forefinger, and squeezed. A small bead of white liquid appeared. "Great! This is the foremilk! You've been doing a good job with your pumping!"

Sam and Max watched, speechless.

She grabbed the roll of tape and one of the lengths of plastic tubing, and started taping it to my nipple.

"We're going to go get a snack." Sam almost shouted it as he grabbed Max's hand and dragged him out of the room. "What is mommy *doing*?" I could hear Max ask as their footsteps faded down the hall. My milk was still coming in, and Judy had suggested ordering this supplemental feeding system to keep the baby from getting frustrated during these first weeks. It was itchy and it definitely felt unnatural – which sort of defeated the purpose – but I was willing to do anything to make this work. If I was going to be missing work and I could feed this baby for free, then I would tape tubes to my chest as long as I had to.

During the afternoon, I checked my phone and found that I had missed several calls from clients. I called them as I held the baby, explained what was going on, and was surprised when – after issuing a curt congratulations and marveling over the turn of events, they expected me to work. As I rocked and took notes on my lap with a free hand, the phone sandwiched between ear and shoulder, I wondered if any other mothers in the maternity ward were closing sales within hours of their child's birth. It jarred me, and yanked me back to reality. I had a brand new baby, and the last thing I wanted to do was take calls – but I also had a *new baby* and new babies are *expensive*. So I steeled myself, and got to work.

For the next two days, I sat in the hospital on pins and needles. The papers had been signed, and our lawyer was filing them with the court, but I was a little fuzzy about whether the parents could still change their minds – which was my worst nightmare. Despite our concerns about bonding, I had almost completely forgotten about the fact that I hadn't given birth. I was so busy breastfeeding and answering the phone to all of the congratulations that it sort of slipped my mind. But every time the door to the little room behind the nurse's station opened I would jump and hold the baby close, wary of anyone who might try to take her away. The first night, after Sam had taken Max home for bed, I asked Lori to come and see the baby. The hallway outside was bustling with proud new fathers and excited older siblings - I wanted to have a visitor while I was in the maternity ward, like a "real" new mother. Having Lori be buzzed in as my "mom", and come into the room with flowers and a huge grin on her face to coo over my baby was another experience that further reinforced my maternal instincts. At that moment, I was just like every other mother on the floor during visiting hours.

In the morning and evening the nurses would take Lucy for an hour to run tests or get some blood, and I took that opportunity to return phone calls or brush my teeth. The rest of the time I sat contentedly in that tiny room, usually alone, staring at my daughter or out the window as I rocked for hours in the wooden chair, listening to the country station on a small radio in the corner. A song kept playing, over and over again on heavy rotation: "Love, Your Baby Girl." And I would sit and rock our baby girl and watch my teardrops roll through her wisps of hair. I wasn't supposed to spend the night, but because I was breastfeeding I insisted on being allowed to stay so that I could feed her. Sam sweetened the deal by arriving on the floor two or three times a day with an armload of food for the staff – pizza at night, donuts in the morning, fruit and cookies and energy bars - whatever he could think of. The nurses kept me hidden in the little room behind their desk, warning me to keep quiet and not let anyone know I was there. "Don't draw attention to yourself! And DON'T LEAVE." they warned me. "Security won't let you back in!"

It turned out that we definitely hadn't needed the car seat right away - the baby wasn't allowed to go home the first day, or the next. They needed to "observe" her, the doctor told me. He was vague about how long we would have to stay. The 24 hour observation period stretched into a third day and I was getting annoyed. I wanted to go home, take a shower, and start nesting. Sam had gone out and purchased a bassinet – assembling it with Max while I spent that first long night on the futon behind the nurses' station. By the second day, my questions got more persistent. Why couldn't I leave? They were waiting for some mysterious test results. There was still some paperwork to fill out.

Finally the pediatrician came to see me. He had a woman with him, in a suit – which is very unusual in Hawaii. He introduced her as the hospital's representative. I figured it had something to do with the adoption, and for a moment, I was truly frightened. Were they going to take her away from me?

"No, no. Not at all." He was quick to reassure me. "We are running some tests, because we got some inconclusive results the first time."

"Results for what?" I sat nursing the baby while we talked, trying to steady my shaking hands by smoothing the blanket around her ears.

He looked uncomfortable. "So, you're breastfeeding? Wow. Um, okay. I'm not sure if…….well. Listen. We're waiting on her test results for HIV."

Everything stopped. Even my breathing. The only thing I was aware of was the baby feeding, and the clock, whose tick was now a deafening "CLACK" with every passing second.

"HIV? Really?"

"Yes, we got an inconclusive test result, so we are waiting for something more definite. And, just, you need to know, because you're breastfeeding and-"

"I need to know because she's my *daughter*."

"Yes, of course, of course. So, we have been following the protocol for babies with possible HIV infection – she is on an antiretroviral, which we give her twice a day.........."

I heard "antiretroviral" and I froze. This was serious. This was really happening. I hammered him with questions: risk factors, percentage of false positives, why the results might be inconclusive. Finally, exhausted, I put the baby on my shoulder and started to burp her. "Well, whatever the results, she's still going home with me. And I want to leave."

The doctor and the lawyer were both visibly relieved. "Oh good. So nothing changes, then."

"What? No. Absolutely not. This is my baby. And if she has HIV, then we'll deal with it. We'll get her the medication she needs. We'll take her to specialists. Whatever we need to do."

Reassured that I wasn't going to abandon the baby in the nursery or sue them if I contracted HIV from breastfeeding because I hadn't been informed, they left quickly. I laid the baby down in her bassinet and picked up the phone. I may have seemed confident when they told me, but in reality I was moments from losing control.

When Sam answered the phone, I explained what was going on. I cried. I paced. I stared out the window while he reassured me that it would all be fine. "Call John," he suggested. "He can explain."

That was a really solid idea.

"John," I said when he picked up "tell me what to do if Lucy has HIV."

"Why do you think she has HIV?" He spoke carefully. John was up on all of the latest treatments - he was a gay man fully aware of HIV risks and treatments. He was also the only person I could call who would provide me with a reality check and some solid information, instead of an emotional response and a bunch of third-hand misinterpreted quotes from the latest issue of Time magazine.

"Her tests are inconclusive. She had a positive test and then a negative test when they retested, so now they need to get a third test result."

"It's okay. Even if it's positive, it's gonna be fine - they are making huge strides in HIV treatments, especially when they catch it early like this. Is she on any meds?"

"Yeah, they just told me that they've been giving her a cocktail of antiretrovirals twice a day. I didn't know. They couldn't disclose it until the legal paperwork was filed or something like that."

"It's okay," he said again. "It's going to be just fine. We have to wait for the test results. They are doing everything they can – which isn't much." I could hear him lean back in his chair and exhale. "So, how is she? How are you? Besides this, of course. All the paperwork going through all right?"

"Yeah, that's all been great. Everything is already filed. I just want to get the hell out of here already."

"So when can you leave?"

"I have no idea. Soon, I hope." Lucy started to cry, and I tucked the phone under my chin to pick her up.

"Oh, I can hear her! Listen, you go take care of that baby. There isn't a damn thing you can do about anything, so just love her and ignore everything else."

"Okay. Hey, thanks."

"Call me later, when you get the test results. Okay?"

"Yep. Absolutely."

I set the phone down and unbuttoned the front of my shirt, attaching a small bottle of formula to the plastic tubes taped to each breast. "You still hungry sweetheart?" A nurse popped through the door. "Are you two ready to go home?"

I grinned up at her. "I've been packed since yesterday."

"I know, I know. Okay, well, I've got the paperwork signed from the doctor, so just a few more things to take care of. Call Sam......you guys can leave soon. I need to explain about the meds, too. You are going home with them. They are really expensive, so you want to be sure you don't waste any." She was visibly relieved. They had all known about the HIV, and I learned later that the nurses had INSISTED that someone tell me what was going on. There had been real concern that we might change our minds and not go through with the adoption once we knew, but that thought had just never even crossed my mind.

It is bizarre now, to think that I had been so concerned about bonding. Concerned about how it would feel to hold someone else's child in my arms. As soon as I held her, I realized:

I wasn't holding someone else's child in my arms. This was my child.

Chapter 10 Settling In

The minute we pulled into the driveway with Lucy, I felt a huge wave of relief. It suddenly felt real, to be home, with two children. There was a lot to do - besides a bassinet waiting for us in the living room, and some freshly washed t-shirts I had pulled down from the attic a few weeks before "just in case" I had done nothing to prepare. We found ourselves standing in an almost empty nursery, without all of the accessories Babies R Us would lead you to believe are necessary for parenting a newborn child.

It was refreshing, actually, to not be tripping over bouncy seats and trying to find the floor space for a swing. I was compelled to take a trip to Old Navy to buy some pink, frilly clothes, and by the end of the first night home word had spread. Our next door neighbor brought over a baby book. Friends began arriving hourly with gifts, new and used, to welcome our newest family member. A shower was planned, more gifts were received, and Lucy was thoroughly celebrated. She had not one, not two, but three itty-bitty bikinis and a faux fur pink pony print diaper cover, several handmade blankets, a quilt with her name embroidered on it, and a stack of ruffled, lacy dresses in floral prints and rosy colors. Not only did I have a brand new beautiful baby – but it was a girl. If her fingernails had been larger than the head of a pin, I would have given her a manicure. I was completely out of my mind with love and girly things.

We took Lucy to her first doctor's appointment when she was 5 days old. She wore a three piece obscenely pink flouncy outfit with a bonnet. I was not messing around. I sat in the room watching her sleep in my arms, and it felt like I was waiting for a jury to come in with a verdict. My pediatrician, who thankfully realized that this was weighing heavily on us, put my mind at ease right off the bat. "She doesn't have HIV." She said as soon as she closed the door. I sat, not moving, but inside I felt the walls crumbling. It was more than just a weight being lifted from my shoulders, it was also the realization that this wasn't some cruel joke being played on us. We really were adopting a baby. A healthy baby girl.

We got the legal paperwork about three weeks before our court date. Sam had filled out the forms in the hospital while I had nursed, and this was the first time I was seeing official documents with my own eyes. I tore the envelope open, eager to see my pending parenthood declared in black and white.

This is when I discovered that my daughter's full name was misspelled on the court papers. Sam had also filled out the forms for the birth certificate, her passport, her social security card, and god knows what else. This was not cool.

I dialed his phone with trembling hands.

"Hey, just got the court papers in the mail."

"Hey, great! Cool!"

"No, actually. Not cool. NOT COOL AT ALL."

"Why? What's wrong?"

The words came out in a torrent. "You misspelled her name. You didn't think to yourself, 'I better look this over to make sure everything is correct before I hand it to my lawyer. WOULDN'T WANT TO MAKE ANY MISTAKES ON THIS REALLY IMPORTANT LEGALLY BINDING DOCUMENT.'? I stopped to catch my breath.

"It was a mistake." He spoke softly. He knew I was furious, but I had hurt his feelings. I tried to swallow my anger. He continued "I'm bad at spelling, what can I say? It was a mistake."

"That is a pretty big mistake."

"I'll fix it."

"THAT IS NOT THE POINT." I was shaking. "What if it puts this whole thing at risk? What if it invalidates something? What if we have to find the birth parents – where ever they are – and say 'Sorry, we made a mistake. Can you sign these again?'

"I'm sure our lawyer can fix it. I'll call him n-"

"WE CAN'T AFFORD TO FIX IT. HER NAME IS SPELLED WRONG."

I hung up. I had thoroughly broken the golden rule, but there was no need to obliterate it. He got the point. And when Sam called to plead his case, our lawyer was able to submit corrections and have them added on to the court documents before everything was finalized. Sam insisted that the lawyer had been the one to make the mistake in his filing, and when we began receiving all of her other paperwork, the name was spelled correctly. Sam had the good sense not to be smug about it, and I had the decency to never bring it up again. Besides, we had a brand new baby and a 4 year old – we didn't really have time to dwell on anything. There was a lot to do, and I had started planning a trip back to the mainland with the kids.

In the time between her birth and our court date, we lived in a strange sort of reality. Lucy was our daughter in every way – but not legally. As the days went by I would forget that she was not my biological child – right up until someone said something about my slim waist, or asked me where Lucy got her hazel eyes or her fair skin. And then reality would come crashing back down around me. Not only was I reminded that my body was unable to sustain a pregnancy, I was reminded that Lucy wasn't "mine". That this could all still be taken away from me. It was like being woken up from a wonderful dream by having someone pull a fire alarm. Each time someone said "You don't look like you just had a baby" I would be reminded – I hadn't. And it hurt. It was jarring to hear the comments. I hadn't really thought about it much before, but it is very similar to people who ask women when they are due, and the women aren't even pregnant. It wasn't compliment, it was upsetting.

As is the way with life lessons and the whole "you don't know until you've walked a mile in my shoes" perspective, I gained some serious insight and compassion during the course of the adoption. One friend's adoption fell through when the birth mother changed her mind. And it was not their first failed adoption. Shortly after we brought Lucy home, a neighbor who was in the midst of adopting a baby girl from Guatemala had to cancel the proceedings. Her husband had been diagnosed with cancer, and their long-anticipated daughter, the one they had visited and held and carried photos of in their wallets – was not going to be theirs after all. I was horrified as I watched these adoptions fall apart. I didn't know what to say or do. I knew how lucky I had been, of course. But this was a worst-case scenario playing out right in front of me. A reminder that nothing – not adoption, not children, not even LIFE should be taken for granted. We were healthy, and we were together. I was determined that it would stay that way, but in the back of my mind I never forgot how fragile it all was. We made the decision to wait for the adoption to be final before taking Lucy to the east coast and introducing her to her grandparents. Once again, my desire not to tempt the fates or "jinx" the adoption was running the show. In the meantime, I sent photos and updates, and called them in the middle of the night during feedings to wax rhapsodic about how smart and lovely she was. My mother had shared my concerns about bonding before Lucy was born, and because she was far away, and not right there experiencing this life-changing event with us, she remained worried that adoption would turn out to be as difficult as fostering had been. On several occasions she mentioned my need to make things more "complicated" and "stressful". Rather than making me feel supported and cared for, I was profoundly angry, as though everyone thought the adoption – just like my infertility and before that my painful periods - was just me being dramatic. Making a big deal out of nothing. No one seemed to understand that it wasn't nothing. That I didn't want to wait years to have children and that I was simply coming to terms with the reality and looking for a solution to a situation that was beyond my control. I wasn't being dramatic, I was being proactive. And it was going pretty well, thanks. Here I was with two beautiful children that I adored, and a loving husband. The process of getting to this point seemed totally unimportant. I was here, now. I had the life I had always wanted. I just needed one last signature from the judge, and I could officially put my "childbearing years" behind me.

Six weeks after we brought Lucy home, we went to court and finalized the adoption.

In the end, we never met her birth parents. Never spoke to them directly or got any letters or medical history or background information or....anything. The birth mother's insurance covered the birth. She did not ask for any financial support and we added the baby to our insurance while the adoption was pending. I hate talking about money, but in this case I want to give you a very clear and specific number.

Our total bill for the adoption was less than $1500.

FIFTEEN HUNDRED. Not fifteen thousand. Or Fifty thousand.

"SEE," Sam said as he sat in the lawyer's office filling out the check. "We *totally* would have had the money to get her name changed." I glared at him.

I will tell you right now: most adoptions don't go like this. In fact, I would estimate that 99.99 percent of adoptions do not even vaguely resemble our experience. And I know that we never considered a private adoption because we were terrified of the expense. But the fact is, it doesn't have to be that way. It doesn't have to cost tens of thousands of dollars.

When you adopt a child from foster care, the cost of the adoption is usually paid by the state. That meant it was in our budget, and was the reason why we signed up in the first place. I just didn't see the point in bankrupting ourselves – whether it was paying for an adoption, or fertility treatments – in order to have a child. Because if we went broke becoming parents, how were we going to support the children once we had them? I didn't think it was a good idea to start our life as a family saddled by debt and the stress that goes along with it.

Just one of the many signs that this was "meant to be" is that we were able to afford it. And when we walked into the courthouse that day and saw our beloved attorney in his rumpled suit sitting on a bench outside family court, I just wanted to cry with gratitude. Because he hadn't charged us some ungodly sum to file papers, we had been able to have a second child. Though to be honest, the minute I held Lucy in my arms I would have sold an organ to pay for the adoption.

The whole bonding thing that I had been concerned about was never an issue – from the moment I held her in my arms she felt comfortable there. And I just never even thought "This is not my biological child." She smelled like my child, I knew her cries, I soothed her and fed her and slept with her curled up in my arms. Max responded just like any new big brother would – guarded curiosity. Sam, I think, had been the one most concerned about bonding. And in the early days, I tried to leave him with her as often as possible. I wanted him to learn about her, to spend time holding and rocking her, feeding her and changing her and meeting her needs so that he – and Lucy – could see that he was, indeed, her father.

I worried that the day would come when she asked questions about why she was given up for adoption. That she would think that, somehow, she wasn't wanted. But I realize now that there can be no question - she was wanted. We wanted her. I wanted nothing more than to be a mother - and no mother ever wanted a baby more than I wanted her. And in more ways than one, she was an answer to all of my prayers. When she was 8 months old, I had a hysterectomy. I was done trying to get pregnant – and after this incredible adoption experience I was sad that we had spent so much time and money trying to conceive. I was relieved to close the chapter on my childbearing years.

Chapter 11 Big Kids

We took an extended break from foster parenting after Lucy was born. Sam was working a new schedule, and the first year of Lucy's life was a sort of dream. We moved to another town, and spent the next year renovating the very small house we now lived in. We enrolled Max in kindergarten and watched Lucy breeze past milestone after milestone, reveling in our good fortune. I wanted to focus on our newly expanded family, but I also wanted to take a step back from the stress and drama that can come with raising a foster child.

Foster parenting is like co-parenting with a huge government bureaucracy *and* the most horrible ex in the world - simultaneously. The social workers try to make this as bearable as possible, but the bottom line is that there are rules and guidelines, and you have to follow them even if you don't agree with them. It can come up in many unexpected ways. For instance, co-sleeping is absolutely not allowed – which makes sense until it is 3am and you are up for the second feeding of the night and you are practically asleep on your feet. At that point, the idea of lying down in bed with the baby starts to sound really nice. Lucy slept right between us in our bed for months, just like Max had before her.

When you are a foster parent, you can't do that.

And while you have control over what happens in your own house, you don't have any control over what happens when they go for visits, which can be in direct conflict with your own rules and ideals.

And as hard as it is for YOU, it is that much harder for the kids in foster care.

One of the issues that I worried about the most, and have had the least trouble with, is seeing the kids after they have gone back to their parents. Most of the time, I just don't see them. Or I don't recognize them if I do. On such a small island, I always find that kind of surprising – I don't know if we've just been lucky, or if it really isn't a problem. But the one time that I did come face to face with a former foster child, I was totally freaked out – just as I thought I would be. Maybe my reaction was that extreme because the foster child I ran into was Faith. And she was 8 months pregnant.

I had Lucy in the carriage, she was a few months old at that point and Faith leaned over to stare at her in shock, as I stood there staring at HER in shock. "You had a *baby*?" she asked incredulously.

"No, we adopted her. You on the other hand, are DEFINITELY having a baby."

She looked up, sheepishly. She had full custody of Sophia again, and her restraining order against Sophia's father was clearly not being enforced: he was the father of her unborn child as well. We chatted briefly, and I made my way out of the store and headed straight for the car. I was glad to see Faith working. I hoped that she was getting the support that she needed, and I was relieved that she hadn't gotten pregnant on my watch. I wondered how that would be handled – did a lot of teenagers in foster care have babies? It made sense, in a way, but when Faith came to live with us, the social workers had talked about it as though it was highly unusual and they didn't really have precedent or protocol for a pregnant teenager in foster care.

Clearly, Faith was exhibiting a need for some sort of call to action. I wondered if it was possible to require minor teenagers in state custody to be on birth control. It didn't seem legal, but it also seemed like the only reasonable thing to do. Under the very best of circumstances, teenagers were going to make terrible decisions. And the teenagers in foster care seemed more vulnerable than the teenagers with supportive, loving, involved parents and consistent rules at home.

As I put Lucy in the car and leaned over to kiss her tiny nose, I reminded her that she was NOT going to be having sex – never mind having babies - until she was at least 25. You should be old enough to be responsible for a rental car before you can be responsible for another life. I was glad to be a few years away from having a teenage daughter – I definitely wasn't ready yet.

One day, out of the blue, our CPS worker Henry called. "Hey, your license is expiring. Did you finish those extra bedrooms yet? Want to renew it?"

"Sure!" I said. I felt….. obligation is the wrong word. I felt indebted to the system that had, in a very roundabout way, led us to our daughter. I felt like I had been given a huge gift, and that I needed to, if not pay it back, at the very least pay it forward.

My first opportunity came about six months later.

Kamaile arrived after school, holding her older sister's hand and crying as they followed the social worker up the steps. This was not the first time they had been taken from their mother, but in the past they had gone to stay with relatives, and they had been able to stay together. This time, she would be separated from her sisters, and living with strangers. My heart broke for her. There were three sisters, and Kamaile was the youngest, at 10 years old. The middle sister was on a school trip, and her older sister wanted to meet us, be there when Kamaile was dropped off and get her settled before going to stay at a friend's house. Kamaile was wearing her school uniform, and carrying a backpack. They had come straight from school. She was moving in with nothing but the actual clothes on her back.

Their mother was a drug addict, their father had died, their family was large and far-flung, and not all of them lived in homes that met state guidelines for foster parenting. One family member didn't have running water. Another didn't have separate bedrooms. A few had so many other children already living under one roof that it wasn't possible to give them custody of any more. Kamaile would be sharing Lucy's bedroom – Lucy was two and a half now, and happy to have a roommate.

My biggest hesitation about having a school-age child sharing a room with one of my kids was that, if they had been exposed to abuse, I might be putting my children in danger, either by having the abusive family members show up at the house, or at the hands of the foster children themselves. Children who have been sexually abused, in particular, were good at being very secretive and I was concerned about that. I had been assured numerous times by several social workers that Kamaile had not been abused, she had been *neglected*, and that my children's safety would not be at risk. I felt confident that with enough love and care, all of the children in our home would be able to thrive.

Kamaile loved Lucy's pink girly bedroom and the big double bed she would have all to herself. We went out and bought her clothes, underwear, a new pair of shoes, and a gaudy t-shirt she loved that said "Mom's Little Princess". I kept my opinions to myself about the shirt, and the message it carried splashed across the front in glittery letters. If it helped Kamaile get through the next few weeks, she could wear that t-shirt 24-7. I was sure her mother, if she ever got sober enough to see straight, would love it.

We also got a large box of lice treatment, which the social worker had recommended as she left that afternoon. I would have appreciated the heads up earlier in the day, but really, what was I going to say? The idea of making a fuss because a foster child had lice seemed really inappropriate. Lice was the least of this child's problems, and easily remedied.

Or so I thought.

We battled lice for the entire time Kamaile lived with us. It was not her fault, she was exposed to them at school, and she was exposed to them every time she went to her family home for a visit. When her belongings were dropped off a few days after she arrived, they were all in garbage bags, and they were just crawling with bugs of all kinds – most of it had to be thrown away, unfortunately, but we sat out in the yard one day and picked through the lot, pulling out some bras and shorts and then washing them in hot water and running them in the dryer for hours hoping to de-louse them.

Other than the lice, everything went so smoothly. We adored Kamaile, she was sweet and lovely and grateful for even the smallest things, like dinner each night with the family and a big clean bathtub to soak in. She was thrilled to have Max and Lucy to play with, and because she was used to having a lot of siblings and cousins around she was patient and kind with these younger kids following her around. However, as time went on and the state began to increase her visits home, she came back repeatedly with lice – including the weekend before Thanksgiving.

I discovered the latest infestation a few days after she had returned from her visit – we had followed our by now usual routine of using the lice shampoo upon her return – I didn't tell her what the shampoo was for, because I didn't want her to feel uncomfortable or embarrassed – I told her it was a scalp treatment that we all had to do once in a while – and indeed, we were all using the shampoo following her family visitations, after several problems with finding lice in the car and on the sofa. None of us had found lice on ourselves, but I figured a quick shampoo treatment "just in case" made sense. It was better to be safe than sorry. Turns out, I shouldn't have been relying on the shampoo alone to kill the darn things.

The night before Thanksgiving I was giving Lucy a bath, and I saw something race across her scalp. I tried not to scream. I ran my fingers along her head making a part as I went, and I saw one, two, three……ugh. This was not good. We had 25 people coming over for Thanksgiving dinner the next day, and Lucy definitely had lice. Sam was working that night, so I ran to the closet for a new bottle of the treatment shampoo, and one of the combs that had been piling up on the shelf.

After about three minutes of trying to work the comb through Lucy's waist-length curls, I realized this was going to be a real problem. I left her soaking in the tub, and ran to their bedroom, stripping the beds and putting everything in enormous black garbage bags, which I tied shut and threw outside on the porch. I ran back to her room and sprayed every surface with some sort of treatment spray that had come with the shampoo. Then I went to find Kamaile, handed her a bottle of shampoo and sent her to the shower. While she showered I checked Max, who was clear. Since he had a buzz cut I hadn't been too worried about him before. But now, I decided to shampoo and comb him real quick just in case – while Kamaile and Lucy were soaking. I was pretty naïve about how insidious lice are, and I was starting to realize that I needed to be very thorough. As he sat in the bathroom with the shampoo on his head, reading a book out loud to his sister who sat in the tub with HER hair foaming and hopefully killing all the livestock running around in there, I went through the house methodically, spraying everything. I burned through three cans, and then ran outside and threw a roach bomb in the car, hoping that it might do the trick on lice too. I came back in the house and checked on Kamaile, who was just finishing up. I told her to put her clothes directly into the washing machine, and added everyone else's for an extra-long hot cycle.

I called Sam, gave him the heads up (no pun intended) and asked him to bring home bombs for their bedrooms, the car he was driving, the bathrooms, and to buy a few more bottles of shampoo and spray – I had used up our supply.

Then, with everyone rinsed and sitting in a row on the floor wrapped in towels and wearing pajama pants and tank tops, I went down the line: parting and combing and rinsing, massaging tea tree oil on scalps and holding a flashlight to their heads to be sure I had gotten everything I could. Everyone went to sleep on pillowless beds sealed in waterproof plastic mattress bags covered with whatever blankets I could find, their hair greasy and wrapped in pillowcases.

Before I fell into bed, I gave myself a treatment, changed our sheets and threw them on the porch with the kids' towels, and then set off the bombs Sam had brought home, one in each bathroom and one in the second car.

Thanksgiving morning dawned early, the kids were sent outside for another head check and an extra dose of tea tree oil, while Sam crawled around their bedrooms spraying and wiping everything down, pulling party clothes out of their room then sealing them shut and setting off the bombs in there just to be safe. Each kid got an extra shampoo, the furniture got an extra spray, and then I turned the oven on. As tempted as I was to stick my head in there, I had Thanksgiving dinner to cook.

The day went off without any further problems. I did a ton of laundry and kept my eyes peeled for any sign of a problem, but Lucy was the only kid who had seemed to have actual lice on her head, and she was clear now so I felt pretty confident that it was safe to have company.

The following week, after another visit with her relatives, I noticed Kamaile scratching behind her ear.

I called the social worker. "Listen," I began. "I hate to make a fuss, and I know it's no one's fault. But Kamaile has lice. Again. I can't deal with this anymore. It is making me crazy. My head itches all the time, I am constantly spraying everything with chemicals and my poor kids have had their scalps examined so many times they are afraid to scratch their head because it always results in everyone getting shampooed and combed. This isn't working. It's too much."

The social worker explained that Kamaile needed to visit her family as they moved her towards reunification. I agreed, but explained that I had always said that we could be foster parents as long as it didn't negatively affect our own kids. This was crossing a line. It seemed like such a little thing, until you were going through the process of delousing for the third time in a month. I just couldn't keep it up for much longer. Could they talk to Kamaile's family about the lice problem? Or have visits take place somewhere else, maybe?

We were at an impasse. The social worker decided to have Kamaile move to her grandmother's house full time that week, instead of doing the move gradually.

I was sad to see her go, but also relieved to know that she was reunited with her sisters, and that I could stop spending a small fortune on lice treatments.

had been the one to take custody and said she would reassure the daughter that Kalei was in good hands. "She's little," the doctor assured me, "but her Apgars were 8 and 9, and she's strong."

On the fourth night, when she was just 5 days old, I stood in the kitchen leaning up against the range giving her a bottle. It was after 11pm, the light over the stovetop was on and it cast a shadow across her face. Suddenly, her head turned sharply to one side, and her mouth opened slightly. She wasn't breathing - she was stiff and I was terrified. I bounced her gently in my arms, cooing in her ear. Her eyes stayed closed, but her body relaxed and her head straightened a she took a breath.

What the hell was that? I was panicked now that the moment had passed. What WAS that? I decided the best thing to do was call 9-1-1. Which I did.

While we waited for the ambulance, Sam held her in the dim light studying her every move while I ran in a panic around the house trying to locate her information folder showing that we were her custodians, and documenting that any issues arising from drug exposure were not because of anything I had done.

The ambulance pulled up without the sirens, and I came outside holding the baby, Sam following with the file folder. They EMTs opened the back of the ambulance and took her vitals while I gave them her brief medical history. As we sat there, a few people came out of their houses in pajamas, and gathered around the back door of the ambulance. In typical small town fashion, my next-door neighbor was friends with the ambulance driver, so they sat on the back bumper and chatted while the baby was passed back and forth and watched for signs of a second seizure. After about 20 minutes, they told me to take my time and drive her down to the hospital for observation. They didn't want to take her in the ambulance, and that made sense - until they left and I realized that driving her myself meant that I would have to drive 25 minutes with her alone in the backseat. That didn't seem like such a great idea. And I was exhausted - too tired to drive, really. This whole plan seemed crazy.

So I got in the shower to wake myself up, and Sam made me a mug of tea for the drive. I headed to town with several stops along the way to check on Kalei, who appeared to be asleep in her carseat. I would pull off the road and run around to the back, check her pulse, watch her breathe, and then jump back in to drive another few miles. It was like a bizarre Chinese fire drill.

When we arrived at the ER we were led to an exam room so that we could avoid sitting in the waiting room with people who were seriously ill. At her age, and her size, with her prematurity, we couldn't risk her catching even the most minor cold.

I lay back on the gurney with Kalei asleep in my arms, and eventually we dozed off. At about 3am we were transferred to pediatrics for the night. I left messages for her social worker and the next morning I got a call back "Why didn't you call the 24 hour hotline?" he asked. "You didn't need to stay with her!"

I was stunned. This was another reality check: I was expected to take care of these children as if they were my own but if there was a complication the State seemed to expect me to walk away. I was confused, but I was also infuriated. This poor baby was 5 days old, drug exposed, separated from her mother, and had just had a seizure. And they expected me to ditch her in the Emergency Room? I'm sure if I had said that out loud they would have thought I was over-reacting, but that was how it felt to me. I was responsible for this child, until I wasn't, apparently - but I had no idea where that line was.

And just like our experience with the breastfed baby, I questioned whether the children's best interests were really coming into play here.

This was when I began to realize that I simply could not keep these foster children at arm's length. They clearly needed someone on their side, a pseudo-parent, to be sure everything was going to be okay. The social workers were well-intentioned, but they carried heavy caseloads and couldn't possibly keep up with all of the minute details of each child. And I couldn't keep myself from getting emotionally involved. I would never think of leaving a newborn baby in a hospital emergency room. That was just ridiculous.

As I sat pondering all of this and rocking the baby to the rhythm of the heart monitor, the phone rang. It was another social worker, calling to tell me that he was leaving the courthouse with the birthmother's

146

husband – while paternity was yet to be determined, he had been granted custody of Kalei. They were on their way to the hospital, and I was free to go. I should probably hurry, actually. They would be there shortly and he was very anxious to see the baby. It might be awkward, and there were privacy issues.

I looked down at the sleeping angel in my arms. I stood up slowly, lay her in the crib, gathered my belongings, and walked out of the room without looking back. I stopped by the nurse's station to let them know what was going on, and they greeted the news with a mix of resigned acceptance and sympathy. "I'm sorry" they said. "Thank you for staying with her."

"I wouldn't dream of leaving her alone. Please make sure she's okay. I'll be worried."

A few offered me hugs as they went back to work. I made my way to the elevator and down to the parking lot. Once back in my car, I sat for a moment and let my head fall back against the head rest. I had been awake for over 24 hours, and my second wind was long gone.

I drove home slowly, and Sam – who had taken the day off of work to get the kids to school - greeted me at the door with a long hug. "You okay?" he asked.

"Yep. It's not me you should be worried about."

"Honey," he said with his face buried in my hair "it's you I worry about the most."

That has been our shortest placement to date, but the memories have stuck with me the longest. 5 days with an angel. For a while, I got updates from time to time through the grapevine, but I haven't heard anything in a while. I think about Kalei often.

Chapter 13 Unplugged

Sam and I are both people that can handle hospitals and emergencies and remain fairly calm. Needles don't bother me, and blood doesn't freak me out (though broken bones send me running for the hills for some reason). So when Henry, our case worker from CPS, called and asked if we could take a particularly difficult case – an infant with a complicated medical history - I didn't blink.

The details were fuzzy. The baby was on another island, and I would have to fly there to pick him up. Mano was a super preemie, and needed supplemental oxygen. Because no one at CPS has medical training, and because I certainly don't have any medical training, it was hard to prepare adequately for this placement. I would have to fly over to the hospital where Mano was being cared for, and meet with his medical team to figure out what I needed before I brought him home. The first thing I had to address was getting time off of work. In those days I was waiting tables full time at night, and taking this case was going to mean handing the baby off every evening at 5 and then rushing to work by 5:30. I talked with Sam, who was willing to give it a shot, and I worked out an emergency plan with my co-workers at the café to cover my shifts if I got stuck at the hospital longer than planned, or if the case ended up being more complicated than I anticipated. I wanted to work, and we needed to have me working, so I took a deep breath and believed that somehow it would all go smoothly. I went shopping for the smallest clothes I could find, and boarded a plane with a diaper bag and a car seat.

But when I landed at the airport and found my way to the hospital, the doctors made it clear: Mano wasn't ready to leave. When he *was* ready, he wasn't leaving without a tank of oxygen. And flying with oxygen was something else entirely. I needed special equipment for that, but no one was exactly sure what that equipment was. I was given the name of a medical supply company near my house, and some paperwork about the machines we would need at home. And then I met the baby. Now, Mano might have been a super preemie at birth, but this kid was now 4 months old and enormous. He was bloated with steroids, but he was also long-limbed and solid – I looked at the preemie clothes I had packed and giggled, then put them back in my bag. I was going to need size 3-6 month clothes, and size 3 diapers, that was for sure.

I flew home empty-handed, reminded of the nights I had left my own son in the hospital after his surgery while I went across the street to get something to eat. It's a feeling of guilt, and regret, and sadness that you have left a baby alone in the hospital – even for just a short time. I was motivated to get the necessary equipment together, and get myself back as soon as possible so that I could bring him home. I also spent hours scrubbing the house, removing any signs of dust or cobwebs or anything else that might make it harder for him to breathe.

When he did finally get released, I was there – fully prepared for anything that could possibly happen. I had a stroller with an oxygen tank in the basket underneath, and a small carry-on with formula and diapers. I also had an enormous roller suitcase full of medical equipment – tubing, masks, filters, some sort of pump-thing, and assorted other items that had been in his hospital room and the nurses had handed to me as I packed. I am sure the sight of me chugging through the airport dragging my suitcase and pushing a stroller that looked for all the world like a rolling NICU was unnerving for other passengers. It was unnerving for me – so much so that I have blocked out large portions of that evening.

I do remember sitting in the departure lounge with the baby asleep in my arms under the fluorescent lights. Several people came up to ask questions, or pat his head, or exclaim over his chubby cheeks – they didn't know those cheeks were a side-effect of the steroids, and not simply the sign of a well-fed baby. It was late, I was tired, the equipment was heavy and I was nervous about flying with it. I was leaving his oxygen tank with the gate agent as we boarded, flying with supplemental oxygen that was onboard the plane, and then another tank would be waiting for me when we landed. There were so many things that could go wrong – and I just kept thinking "What have I gotten myself into?" This was becoming a familiar refrain.

It turns out that I had gotten myself into quite a predicament, but the flight itself went really smoothly. By 10pm, I was home, monitors flashing on mute, Mano asleep in the bassinet next to my bed. The trouble began within about 30 minutes. He used supplemental oxygen 24 hours a day, and he was also hooked up to a "pulse-ox" which is a small tab sensor that I had to keep taped to his tiny, chubby little toe, to keep track of his pulse and oxygen levels. Surprisingly, that was the detail that caused me the most stress. I learned very quickly that keeping a small tab taped to an infant's toe is not as easy as it sounds. Babies – even sick ones – kick and twist and rub their little feet together. Poor Mano was constantly getting twisted up in his tubes and wires, and every time the sensor came loose – even in the slightest – an alarm would sound, startling all of us. The alarm was most jarring in the middle of the night, which was also, unfortunately, when it seemed to go off the most often. I would jerk awake hour after hour, night after night, fumbling in the dark to try to reattach the sensor tab without turning on a lamp.

I tried everything to keep that sensor attached to him securely. Swaddling, socks, modified finger cots, and every kind of tape I could find. I stopped just short of duck taping his entire foot. His skin was raw from having adhesive on it all the time, and we went through two or three sensors a day. Another issue was keeping the oxygen prongs in his tiny, button nose. That involved tape too, but the skin on his face was even more delicate than the skin on his toe, and I was always anxious when I went to remove it, for fear that I might hurt him. He was surprisingly calm about having the prongs in his nose – probably because he had been wearing them since birth and didn't know life without them.

The oxygen tanks were comical. I had a few fire extinguisher-sized tanks in the car that were easy to stash in the stroller. But standing at about 4 feet tall, the house tanks were anything but discreet. There was one in the bedroom and one in the living room, plus a backup for fast access. There were a few more on the porch. It gave the impression that I was about to inflate a lot of balloons. All I needed was a clown or two - god knows the house was a total circus, with beeping machines competing for space amid all of the brightly colored baby gear. Medical equipment competed with the plastic toys: their flashing lights, alarms, and cheerful music were scattered across every surface.

Mano was on a very specific regimen of steroids received via a face mask, followed by oral medication. So in the morning, once we had gotten through the nebulizer treatments, I began the battle of wills that is getting a baby to swallow medicine. He inevitably spit and drooled it all over both of us and the surrounding area – I learned to tuck a blanket around him first, and used it to mop off everything afterwards. The steroids contained in the breathing treatments, combined with the bright pink medicine I had to convince him to take, left both of us sticky and stressed out. I had been told that a side effect of his medication was "restlessness". I quickly learned that this restlessness meant that he was twitchy and cranky for several hours after each dose. He couldn't sleep, or relax – and it made for a very long morning and evening when he was both exhausted and strung out. When I got close to the end of the bottle of medicine I had brought from Oahu, I called his pediatrician to get a refill. He called it in to the local drugstore, and I went over to pick it up one afternoon. That is when I learned that the refill couldn't be filled at any random corner pharmacy. It had to be mixed by a compounding pharmacy – there was only one of those on island, and it turned out they had to special order one of the ingredients. I spent the next two days carefully rationing out the remaining medication, making sure that even the bits that dribbled out of his mouth were accounted for. He needed every drop.

I was a wreck. The whole "compound pharmacy" had been a total newsflash for me – I had never even heard of such a thing. And between the monitors interrupting my sleep every 15 minutes, and the level of care Mano needed on a constant basis, plus never being able to leave the house without several tanks of oxygen while trying to keep our day-to-day life relatively "normal" for Max and Lucy, I was completely stressed out. It felt like I was bouncing from one crisis to another. Even the most well-planned outing had the potential for drama: one day we got stuck waiting longer than expected at the doctor and I had to race to the medical supply before they closed to pick up a fresh tank of oxygen for the drive home. It was just another level of being responsible for a child's wellbeing that I hadn't experienced before.

On the bright side, Mano was a pleasure to have around. He was such a sweet happy baby – and was not born drug-exposed, so he had none of the withdrawals or complications associated with that. He had simply been born very prematurely. His mother had been airlifted – in labor – to a hospital with a NICU, and he had spent many months in the hospital after his birth. Once he had passed his actual due date, he was released into his parents care and had returned home. They struggled to take care of him, and to do so under very extreme conditions. They were living in poverty, several generations under one small roof. English was a second language, and their life did not mesh well with a child on oxygen support. They had trouble operating the equipment. Had trouble keeping the electricity on to run the monitors. Had no air conditioning and lived in the hottest, dustiest, most industrial area of the island. Had trouble understanding what the warning signs were for respiratory distress.

And they were all chain smokers.

When a social worker came to their house and found Mano attached to a completely empty oxygen tank and turning blue while his grandmother attempted to feed him a bottle, he was airlifted back to the NICU and a decision was made that his delicate medical condition could not be managed by his family given their current living arrangements. His parents were going to look for more stable accommodations, and the state would line up the in-home support they would need to care for him successfully. In the meantime, he would live in a foster home - which is when I got the call.

A team of professionals was assembled in the first few weeks that he was with us – working with doctors, nurses, respiratory and physical therapists was all part of caring for Mano. We had frequent appointments and lots of different procedures to follow at home. There were things I learned that I needed to be on the lookout for, signs of a problem, and most importantly the proper use of the equipment he relied on to survive. In my first meeting with the pediatrician, I was the one who relayed much of the information from the neonatologist, and went over the details of Mano's care. The doctor was taken aback by my confidence, and my comfort with the complicated treatment plan. He asked what medical training I had, and I assured him that I had absolutely none - which, in retrospect, seemed to stun him even more. I was unqualified, and very casual about the serious nature of this case.

I didn't think Mano would be with me for long, but it took time for his parents to find a new home that he would be able to live in. While they were looking for a place, he was doing well with us, which was all I could hope for. My birthday rolled around a month or so after he joined our family, and my friends were getting together for a big dinner at the restaurant I worked at. I definitely couldn't leave my teenage babysitter with my two kids plus an infant on oxygen, so Mano came with us, oxygen tanks and all. There was live music that night, and he snoozed in his stroller, a cap pulled down tightly over his ears and the sunshade pulled closed over his seat, leaving him in a quiet cocoon as we laughed and danced and took pictures, checking on him every few minutes to make sure he was still asleep. When he woke up, we passed him down the long table, everyone cooing and cuddling and admiring his long eyelashes and sweet rosebud lips. It was easy to forget how sick he had been – and how sick he still was. He smiled and turned his head to take in the excitement, before eventually tucking his head under my chin and falling asleep on my chest. I sat and held him, feeling him breathing steadily as I patted his back. I felt like we had rounded the corner, together, and envisioned a future where he didn't need the supplemental oxygen and the monitors and medications. He was going to be fine. I just knew it. After that night, I relaxed a little bit. If the alarm went off more than a few times in one night, I turned the volume off. I believed that with peace and quiet and lots of rest, he was going to be better off than if I hovered over him constantly monitoring, and if he was woken up from a sound sleep repeatedly for no reason whatsoever. And every morning he greeted me with a wide grin when I leaned over the bassinet to gather up the tubes and wires and bring him with me to the living room.

And then one day, I heard a cough.

It is hard to explain how a little cough from the back seat could sound so wrong.....but it did. It was more than a cough, of course. It sounded like he was being strangled. There was a strain. He was coughing almost in slow-motion by the time I had pulled the car over and thrown myself between the front seats to check on him. His color was okay, his oxygen tank was full, the oxygen was flowing through the prongs which were still securely in place, but there was this worry I couldn't shake. Something was not right. I hopped out of the car and ran around to the back, climbing over the diaper bag and the oxygen tank to get my ear up to his chest. I could feel his ribs constricting, which I knew was bad. And there was a strange sound that I didn't recognize in his breathing. I sat and stared at him for a while. Maybe I was imagining it. After all, I lived in constant fear that something would go wrong. I could totally be projecting. He might be fine. I increased the flow of oxygen through his prongs and after a few minutes he seemed to relax. Eventually he dozed off, and I drove home and hooked him up to the pulse/ox. The number was a little low, but nothing too alarming. I put him back in the car and headed over to the school to pick up my kids, and called the pediatrician to ask what he thought might be going on. The nurse called me back within moments. "Bring him to the ER."

I was in the carpool line at school. Mano was asleep and not making that noise anymore. I could hear the oxygen hissing gently through the prongs. I got the kids in the car, and swung through McDonalds to get them Happy Meals on our way to the hospital. I had no time to go home and make snacks, but I didn't want to get to the ER and be stuck with a sick baby and two hungry kids indefinitely.

As I pulled out of the drive-thru, my phone rang. It was the hospital. "May I speak to the parent of Mano?"

"This is his foster mom."

"We have a team here waiting for you – where ARE you?"

I was mortified. I had no idea this was a "gather an emergency response team" situation, and wondered why I hadn't been instructed to call an ambulance if the situation was so dire. I had a flash of guilt, a flash of anger, and then both gave way to panic.

I felt like the worst parent ever.

I pulled up in front of the ER and ran around the car opening doors and unbuckling seatbelts and grabbing the oxygen tank to secure in the stroller with the diaper bag. I raced through the doors trailing two kids and some tubing that dangled from the car seat, french fries in my stroller cupholders, Lucy begging me to open her Happy Meal toy, and Max balancing the drinks and his notebook from school. There was a nurse on lookout, and as soon as she spotted me the interior doors swung open and we were ushered through. There was an ER bay open in the back of the room, next to the hallway that led to the radiology department. As they began assessing him, I started signing forms and answering questions from doctors, nurses and administrative staff who were all trying to get a handle on the situation simultaneously. I called Mano's social worker, who jumped in his car and headed over to meet me. Someone sat Max and Lucy down at a small table around the corner, and gave them crayons and packages of graham crackers. They sat quietly, coming to peek in through the curtain every once in a while at the chaos that surrounded the gurney. I went with the baby to get his chest x-ray, and they stayed behind with a nursing student who was charged with keeping them safe, occupied and out of the way while I was gone.

To get a clear and readable infant chest x-ray, babies are strapped into a contraption that looks like a torture device from the 30's but which – I was assured – was the latest technology. The baby is seated on a leather "saddle" that looks sort of like a bike seat. Then a clear plastic case is snapped around their torso, pinning their arms pointing straight up in the air on either side of their head. They are left in this position for several minutes while the x-rays are taken, and Mano screamed the entire time – really, who could blame him.

Before we had even walked back to the ER, we had the answer to the mysterious cough: his lung was collapsed.

I cried. I felt so responsible, and so frustrated. I had done everything I knew how to do, to keep this child safe and well, and when I thought something might be wrong I had stopped at MC DONALDS instead of driving straight to the hospital. The social worker and the doctors reassured me that I hadn't done anything to cause it, and that he would be okay. In an effort to calm myself, I tried to focus on the logistics: Mano was being admitted to the hospital, and I was working the dinner shift. I checked my watch as I was signing the forms to have him admitted overnight. I had an hour and a half to get to work. We kissed Mano goodbye and left him snoozing in his crib while the social worker notified his family. They lived near the hospital, and I knew they would want to stay with him. I was relieved that he wouldn't be alone overnight. I loaded everything into the stroller and headed to the parking lot.

I ran into the restaurant just in time to clock in and seat the first table of the evening. At about 8pm I checked my phone and found a voicemail.

"This is Laura, I am a nurse at the hospital and I am taking care of Mano tonight. We need you to bring his medication."

I was bewildered. It was a hospital. Every time I had ever been admitted to the hospital I had been told NOT to bring my own medication. Didn't they HAVE medication there already? And why didn't they ask me for it when I was there? Or mention it during the admitting process? I called the ward in a panic:

"Hi. This is Mano's foster mother. I am so sorry, I am at work and I can't get to the hospital until probably 11 or so. Maybe later. I wish I had known he needed the medications, I would have had my husband bring them down earlier, but now the kids are asleep and he can't leave the house. Should I call a sitter and have him bring them right away?"

After a few minutes of back and forth, we agreed that I would bring the prescription first thing in the morning. He had been given a lot of medication and breathing treatments to stabilize him in the ER, and he probably didn't need any more that night anyway. The nurse told me he was "restless" and I couldn't even imagine what Mano's "restless" looked like after the super-sized doses of steroids he had received that afternoon. But they needed that special medication he was on - the *hospital* didn't even have the all-important compounding pharmacy needed to make his prescription.

Once again, it was all on me – to know, to prepare, and to advocate and oversee his medical treatment.

The next morning I walked into Mano's hospital room and was surprised to find his grandmother asleep in the bed, with him in her arms. She woke, startled, and I smiled and waved, but she didn't speak

English so we had no way to communicate. I went back out to the nurse's station and handed over all of his prescriptions. They assured me they would call when he was ready to be released, and I assured them that it was totally fine to have his family stay with him in the hospital – as long as they didn't leave with him, of course. The nurses were not amused. The last thing they had time for was keeping Mano on lockdown, but I reminded them that the family had never abused him or hurt him intentionally, and that this was actually an excellent opportunity to show them – over and over again – how to care for him properly. "He's going back to them soon, and they really need all the support and help they can get." The supervisor reluctantly agreed, but reminded me that they were understaffed, and didn't have much time with each patient.

"It's okay," I tried to sound upbeat "every opportunity to learn is valuable!" I sounded like a cheerleader, but in reality I was frustrated. How was his family ever going to learn, if they never spent time with him? A few hours of visitation twice a week was not going to do it – this was an opportunity for them to care for him around the clock with supervision, and honestly it seemed like a win-win scenario. They could bond with him, and at the same time get familiar with his routine. And *I* certainly wasn't the person to teach them all they needed to know about his medical care. I suggested that they get a translator, and the nurse raised an eyebrow, clearly indicating that the last thing they needed was another person to answer to in that hospital room. It was already a parade of social workers, relatives and therapists – Mano's regular schedule at home had followed him to the pediatric ward, and everyone was just now realizing what a task it was to keep his medications and appointments straight. I took a deep breath and headed home to catch up on my laundry and my sleep. I was off-duty for a few days, and I was going to make the most of it.

Sam and I spent the next two days at the beach with the kids. We hadn't been there since Mano had joined our family, for obvious reasons. Oxygen tanks and tubing do not mix well with sand and wind and salt water. Our life, without even realizing it, had changed completely in the past few months. It had changed so profoundly, in fact, that I could not remember the last time we had been to the beach. For a family living in Hawaii with two kids, that is pretty extraordinary. When Mano was released on Monday morning, I went to pick him up with sunburned cheeks and sleepy eyes. I had slept long and hard that weekend, my brain so starved for rest that it felt as though it shut off as soon as the sun set. His family, on the other hand, looked exhausted. Haggard. Spending a weekend in the hospital leaves everyone the worse for the wear, but staying in the hospital with a baby with some pretty serious health problems means that you don't even get crappy rest. You just don't sleep at all. His mother was tearful as I strapped him into his carseat, but she seemed almost relieved to know that he was going to my house, and not back to their two-room cottage filled with six people. I took Mano home and reattached the pulse-ox, turning the volume all the way up. I was resigned to giving up sleep to ensure that I would never have a scare like that again.

The next week we had an Ohana Conference. Ohana is the Hawaiian word for "family", and in Hawaii there are Ohana Conferences scheduled for the biological and foster families of each child, along with the team that works with the child on a regular basis. Everyone who is involved with the child's care and well-being is invited to attend. At the conference, I was informed that Mano's family had finally found a place to live, and that it was over an hour from my home on the other side of the island. I suggested that the baby be transferred to a foster home closer to his family, to help with visitation and eventual reunification. Everyone at the meeting had a different opinion about it – some wanted him to stay with me, some saw that having everyone in the same area would be easier. There was a long conversation, and when I left that day it was still unresolved.

The next morning when I noticed that Mano was coughing again, I decided as I drove back to the hospital that while they decided where he was going to live, the state really needed to address whether having him in a foster home was actually the best place for him to begin with.

The ER admitted Mano again, and I lay on the gurney holding him while I called his social worker. After explaining where I was, and what was happening, I raised the issue with him. "Listen, honestly? I think he needs more care than I am able to give him."

The social worker was quiet.

"A lung collapse is not a small matter, you know that. And what if something happens in the middle of the night and I sleep through the alarm? He needs to be monitored 24 hours a day. The stress of it is too much. It's too much for me, but honestly, I think it is too much for the state to take on, period. This is a huge liability. What if something happens to him in foster custody? It's not out of the realm of possibility."

The social worker decided to call the pediatrician and ask his opinion.

The pediatrician – the same doctor who had been so impressed by the way I handled the case from the beginning, told the social worker that they needed to find a better foster placement. He insisted that I was incompetent and shouldn't be allowed to care for Mano if I wasn't able to handle the possibility of a complication. That he didn't need to be getting panicked phone calls from me on a weekly basis. If I had doubts or concerns, he announced, it would be best to find a new foster home immediately. The baby was not going to be admitted overnight, so they had better move quickly.

The social worker called me to relay the conversation - we were both stunned by the doctor's reaction.

I was frustrated. I really didn't believe that I was doing a terrible job, or over-reacting. And I truly felt that at this point the best place for Mano was in a long-term care medical facility with 24 hour nursing staff. But because his pediatrician asserted that I had shortcomings as a foster parent, and that anyone should be able to handle this case, Mano was transferred to another foster home instead of a nursing facility. The foster parents lived near his family's new home, as we had discussed during the Ohana conference - but we all knew that he was moved because the doctor felt I was not a good choice to care for him full time.

I wasn't able to say goodbye – his new foster parents picked him up from the hospital that night and brought him home, while I hauled the oxygen tanks to the car and drove them back to the medical supply office. I was chided for driving with massive tanks of oxygen in my car, which apparently is very dangerous - yet another piece of information regarding the complexity of this case that I was learning too late.

In the end, Mano was admitted to a nursing home as I had suggested from the beginning. He is – as far as I know – still there. Because I am no longer his custodian, I do not get any updates, nor am I allowed to visit. My part of the case was closed, and in the state's mind I have no need for any further information. It would be an invasion of Mano's privacy.

My case worker Henry called later on that month to reassure me that no one in the CPS office thought I had done anything wrong – I supposed I should have felt grateful, but instead I felt embarrassed that the quality of my work as a foster parent had been debated.

We took a break from foster parenting for about a year after this case. My health had deteriorated and I had another surgery that showed more endometriosis. The hormone replacement therapy appeared to be triggering small pockets of the disease that had been hidden (or microscopic) and new damage was being done. This time, my gallbladder was removed. The surgeons found part of an ovary - probably from one of the cysts that had ruptured, they theorized.

It took me a while to heal. I felt frustrated by doctors in general, and I needed to get some distance from hospitals and appointments. I started doing yoga. I joined a roller derby team. We traveled, and began taking what is now an annual summer trip to see family in New England.

Life went on.

Chapter 14 Baby's First Christmas

It had been over a year since Mano was transferred to a new foster home. I had begun making little comments, here and there, about how it might be time for another baby. Sam was steadfast – he did not want more children. But foster parenting was still on the table – wasn't it? We had kept our license renewed and the baby gear was all tucked away in the attic. We discussed it more and more frequently.

I was ready – more than ready – to take a new case. But Sam was very happy with two kids, everyone out of diapers, $50 cans of formula forever removed from our shopping list. The idea that a foster case could turn to an adoption placement made him nervous.

"Well," I negotiated "if someone just called and offered me a baby, I could say yes, right? I mean, you wouldn't expect me to say no, would you?"

Sam rolled his eyes at my optimism. "You mean, if someone called and offered you ANOTHER newborn baby? Sure. If someone calls you again, out of the blue, and offers you a baby, you can say yes. Absolutely."

In the meantime, we were enjoying the freedom that came as the kids got older and more independent. Max, who was in middle school and fairly responsible, would stay at home from time to time while I ran down the road to town for a few groceries, or to pick up Sam at work. And finally, one night, after a family meeting it was agreed that Sam and I would try going out for dinner and leaving Max and Lucy at home watching a movie while we drove five minutes away. I was a nervous wreck, but at the same time we were all excited at the prospect of not needing to hire a sitter every time we wanted to leave the house without the kids for more than 10 minutes at a stretch. "Call me if you need me." I said sternly before we left. "No fighting. If both of you behave, BOTH of you will get $5 when I get home." They grinned and nodded, and started the movie, settling down on the sofa.

And just like that, we had 97 minutes – one movie's worth - of freedom.

An hour later, we were sitting on a porch in the rain under battered fluorescent lights, laughing with friends. The table was littered with bottles of wine, trays of sushi, and plates of ginger. Our favorite sushi joint was located in a ramshackle plantation house behind a grove of banana trees with a view of the electricity substation. It was the week before Christmas, but Christmas lights were part of the year-round décor. I opened a third bottle of wine and filled the glasses again. We weren't feeling particularly festive, but we were celebrating – the day had been spent moving the kids' school to a new location where it would reopen after the holidays. The whole move had been completed in one day, and we were relieved. It could have dragged on through the holiday break, and none of us wanted that to happen.

The conversation was boisterous, laughing and joking and then my cellphone rang, and everyone quieted down, refilling glasses as I grabbed my phone from behind a bottle of soy sauce. The screen said "State of Hawaii Gov."

I knew exactly what that meant. I looked at Sam and said "Henry's on the phone."

He shook his head and went back to his sushi while I answered. "Hello?"

"Hey. It's Henry. I just called the house but the kids said you were out."

"Hey. Yeah, we're around the corner grabbing dinner. What are you doing working on the weekend?"

"I have a baby for you."

"You always know the right thing to say."

"You're available?"

"Sure. What have you got?"

"Baby boy, born yesterday, positive for crystal meth."

"When do I need to be ready?"

"Tomorrow. He'll be released tomorrow."

"Got it. I'm ready whenever you are."

"Okay, the worker will call you in the morning."

I hung up the phone. Sam and our friends stared at me, mouths agape.

"We're getting a baby tomorrow?" Sam shook his head again, but he was grinning. "I don't know how you do that."

"You're getting a WHAT tomorrow?" Debbie sat there, stunned. Her husband Michael rocked back in his chair and laughed. He and Sam rolled their eyes, Debbie covered her mouth and looked at me, eyes wide. "Who? What? HOW DOES THIS STUFF HAPPEN TO YOU?"

I picked up a piece of sushi and popped it in my mouth. "I think I'm going to need another glass of wine. Sam, we have to go home and unpack the attic."

"Crap." He was not thrilled at the idea of more moving boxes but we had everything in one area of the attic, so it wouldn't be too bad. We finished dinner and headed back to the house, ready to fire up the washing machine and assemble baby furniture.

At around noon the next day, Dude was dropped off by a social worker. His name was not actually Dude, but the first words out of my mouth were "Look at you, little dude!" and the name just stuck. He was wrapped up in an Old Navy pullover fleece jacket, and all that poked out of the top was a hospital hat, his face hidden. I brought him up to the house, unbuckled him, and lifted him up to take his jacket off.

Another tiny baby. He was sound asleep, not waking up as I removed the jacket and hat and lay him down on the sofa to get a good look at him. The social worker grinned. "He's a little one, huh?"

"He sure is, but we've had smaller." I scooped him up and tucked him in the crook of my arm while the worker pulled out some documents for me to sign. She left shortly afterwards, and I sat there in the sunny living room, with a brand new baby weighing in at just over 5 pounds, and a can of formula from the hospital. It was Sunday, six days before Christmas.

Monday dawned cold and bright – even in Hawaii temperatures can drop into the 50's and sometimes as low as the 40's at night at higher elevations. Dude was going to need some fleece pajamas for Christmas. I got the kids up and dressed, tucked the baby deep inside a sling, wrapped both us inside an old floppy cardigan, and headed out to finish our Christmas shopping and get everything to the post office in time for Christmas delivery. As we walked through the stores in our little village, people kept stopping me to ask whose baby I was carrying, or to congratulate me on our new arrival. After years of foster parenting I was used to the confusion by now, and almost wished I could just pin a sign on my sweater that said "three day old foster child (boy) 5 lbs 2 oz" to avoid the stream of questions that were directed at us all morning long.

We were home shortly after noon, Dude still asleep and the kids buzzing with excitement after walking through the stores all decked out for the holidays. We played Christmas music and drank hot cider and watched the baby snoozing in his bassinet. In a show of spectacularly bad timing, I was scheduled to begin a writer's workshop – the first I had ever attended – in two days' time. I had no idea what to do about it. I had lined up our usual teenage babysitter for the week, but she couldn't be left with three kids – one of them four days old. How does one attend a writer's workshop with a newborn? I guess one just muddles through. At least he still slept a lot. As I sat on the couch and pondered my options, the phone rang. My friend Sarah was one of the driving forces behind me actually signing up for the workshop to begin with, and she knew about the new baby. She was determined that it would not affect my attendance, and offered to watch all three kids while I went to the first day's session. I sat back with relief. Once again, everything was falling into place. I wondered what, exactly, I had done to be so fortunate.

That feeling of being fortunate came to a screeching halt the next morning. As I drove down the mountain to take the baby to his first doctor's appointment, my phone rang. I answered it on speaker. It was the baby's social worker, and she was calling to let me know that the biological family was meeting me at the doctor's office.

I was not pleased.

It had been a difficult surrender. When Child Protective Services arrived to the hospital to take custody of Dude, his mother – who had been high on crystal meth at the birth - was upset. Her family was upset. The baby's father was very upset. The social worker – a person who did this for a living and had taken custody of countless children during her career – had been rattled. This definitely did NOT sound like a situation I wanted to get involved with, and I was glad my kids were home with the sitter. There was no getting around it, Dude's family had been told where and when the appointment was, and I was going to meet them – whether I wanted to or not.

As I filled out the paperwork, the social worker arrived, and introduced me to Dude's mother and her family – a brother, a grandfather, and a few other people I did not meet were gathered around her and all of them cooed and smiled at the baby. The father was nowhere in sight. I handed Dude to his mom, Jess, and went back to the registration desk where we spent some time trying to explain his custody arrangement and insurance coverage to the receptionist. Finally, our name was called and Dude's mother headed back to the examining room with me. The social worker headed off to court, leaving me to supervise mom's visit while the rest of the family waited in the lobby. I was terrified – what if she tried to leave with him? Why was I in this situation? Once again, I found myself wondering what I had gotten myself into.

As we sat waiting to see the doctor, I noticed that Jess' behavior was.......odd. She kept sniffing, and didn't seem able to make eye contact. Her arms were covered with scars from cutting, and seeing the baby resting there surrounded by the scars was a poignant reminder of his reality. He was born to a mother who was not able to care for herself, or for him.

When the doctor arrived, Jess asked to have Dude circumcised. I blanched. I definitely did not want to be around for that procedure and I couldn't leave her alone with him. Once again, I wondered why the social worker had left me in charge of this visit. I did not feel like I had the information or authority to be "in charge" – I was just here for a quick 5 day old checkup, not a family reunion/circumcision.

The doctor nipped her idea in the bud. "Circumcising him is the very LEAST of my concerns." He said somberly. He reminded both of us, though only one needed the reminding, that Dude was facing a series of obstacles, and at this point keeping him fed and safe was the most important task at hand. The mother nodded as she stared down at her baby, and it was then that the doctor spotted her scars.

He froze, and then seemed to shake himself out of it. "So, what drugs were you taking during your pregnancy?"

"Crystal" she told him, as though it was something glamorous. He was having none of that. "Meth? What else." It wasn't a question, it was a statement. She admitted to smoking cigarettes, but said she hadn't drank. She seemed almost defensive about it, as though we were completely out of line making such an assumption.

The doctor took the baby out of her arms and laid him down, undressing him and looking him over. "Do you see how small he is?"

He asked her. She nodded silently. "It's because of the drugs. And the cigarettes. Your body is miraculous. It knows exactly how to grow a baby, and you don't need to do anything special – but you absolutely cannot smoke or do ANY drugs when you are pregnant. Otherwise your baby won't grow properly." She wouldn't look up. Her eyes shifted back and forth quickly as she stared at the floor.

He sighed and wrapped the baby back up. "Take him back. I am going to go get the social worker. She is going to talk to you for a minute about the resources we have to help you stop using drugs, okay?" Dude's mom nodded again, eyes still downcast. I picked the baby up and stuck him in the Baby Bjorn.

The social worker bustled in as I tried to gather our belongings together and duck out. She closed the door firmly behind her and blocked my exit. As she began asking Dude's mom all sorts of questions about her mental health and drug use, I was edging towards the door. The social worker was oblivious, and proceeded to violate every single aspect of Jess's privacy as I stood there, horrified. Dude's mother outlined her entire medical history, describing her drug use, the self-harm that escalated after her grandmother's death, her pregnancy and Dude's birth, as I tried to catch the social worker's eye and excuse myself, to no avail. I finally just succumbed. I had already heard everything, and I decided that my best plan was to encourage Dude's mom to get the help she needed. So I asked the social worker for her card, encouraged Dude's mom to call her, took some notes about places she could call for treatment, and thanked the social worker as I stepped around her and opened the door to leave.

Out in the lobby, the family was still waiting. They passed the baby around and hugged him, and then got in their car and drove away while I strapped Dude into his carseat, taking my time and hoping they wouldn't follow me home.

That afternoon I called the social worker and tried to calmly explain that I was not comfortable being left along with the family. That the mother was clearly still using drugs, and that she was also cutting, and how important it was that there be a social worker with her whenever she spent time with the baby. The social worker was not convinced. She insisted that the mother was not a hard core addict. That she was a casual user. That she was going to get clean and take her baby back. That her family was going to support her in that effort.

Her version bore very little resemblance to the reality I had witnessed at the clinic. I hoped that she was right, but in my heart I knew that she was either misinformed, or trying to protect their privacy. I simply repeated that I did not feel comfortable being left along with the mother. I was told that it was unavoidable. That a very important part of the reunification process was having the foster parents and the birth parents communicate and co-parent. The system was changing in response to budget cuts and the department's reaffirmation of the importance of returning children to their biological family. Apparently they were intent on doing so, whether it was in the child's best interests or not. I was livid.

The next day I headed off to the writer's workshop with my laptop and notes. I was so excited to be actually, finally doing something pro-active about my writing – but my excitement was tempered by the reality that – once this workshop was over – I would have very little time in which to write. I had a brand new baby and two children at home, and a new part-time job. My six hours of quiet a few days a week while the kids were at school had just disappeared in the blink of a tiny eye.

And then, that tiny little eye became a very big concern.

At first, I wasn't worried: one morning, his eye was sticky with something that resembled clear snot. His eyelashes would occasionally be stuck together, and I wiped his face clean each time with a damp washcloth as the nurse instructed when I asked her about it over the phone. Probably a blocked tear duct, I was told. Common in newborns, I was reassured.

And I had other more pressing things to worry about, like keeping him swaddled and comforted and encouraging him to stay awake long enough to eat. Dealing with the umbilical cord that refused to dry up, and his constant gas pains. Finding clothes that didn't fall off his five pound frame. God, he was so small those first few weeks. Coming off the drugs, he would cry silent tearless cries, mouth open, head twisting to the side, back arched. But he seemed otherwise healthy until

Christmas Eve morning, when his eye started draining yellow goop and was stuck shut. And then the other eye looked a little weird. By dinner time I was worried enough to call a friend who had been an ER physician, and we agreed that I should bring him to the hospital to get checked out. And so, in the middle of a winter rain storm, with high winds gusting over the island and the puddles gleaming in the streetlights, I wrapped Dude up and took him to the emergency room. He was 8 days old.

Born two weeks early, the blood in his veins coursing with crystal meth and nicotine, he was still six days shy of his due date that night. The idea of taking him to the ER with all of its germs and drama seemed counter-productive, but it couldn't be helped on a holiday weekend. The nurses weighed him, and oohed and aaahed and told him how very beautiful he was, as he farted and grunted and moaned loudly with his mouth agape and his head twisting, as was his way. As it neared midnight and I began to worry about getting home to hang the stockings, he slept quietly on the gurney. I lay next to him reading the newspaper. They took samples of the goop on his eyes and sent it off to the lab: "Could be chlamydia", the doctor informed me solemnly. We left for home shortly after 11pm with a tube of erythromycin ointment, just in time for Santa – it was baby's first Christmas.

I dutifully applied the ointment and warm compresses as I had been directed, and on Christmas morning, we had already committed to a plan for Dude's grandmother to pick him up and take him to her family's house for lunch and presents. She had not been at the clinic for that first visit, and I was not happy that I was once again being asked to interact with the family without supervision. What if they took the baby and didn't come back? Dude's grandmother was also given my cellphone number and email address without my permission in order to get in touch with me over the holiday. I felt helpless and frustrated, totally exposed by the social worker. I was surprised they didn't just give her my home address and tell her to come get him at her convenience.

We met in the Safeway parking lot. Dude's grandmother – maybe a few years older than me - was driving a new minivan with booster seats in the back. She was nicely dressed, her hair recently highlighted and her nails manicured. Dude's mother Jess appeared to be sober, and was dressed in clean clothes, not the ill-fitting t-shirt and cutoffs she had worn when I met her at the clinic. Maybe her drug use really was a random, ill-timed teenage mistake? I was bewildered. Why was the baby in foster custody when his grandmother appeared completely able to care for him? What was going on? I reminded myself that appearances could be deceiving. There had to be a very good reason that the baby was with me.

I couldn't help but wonder what it was.

The visit went off without a hitch, the baby returned to us clean, fed and sound asleep. But despite his mother and grandmother taking him home for the holiday and introducing him to all of his relatives, there was still no update on his custody status. The social worker was in contact with several relatives – maternal and paternal - and trying to get one of them certified to be able to take temporary custody, but no one seemed particularly enthusiastic about dropping everything to care for a brand new baby. I had a sneaking suspicion that there might be some hesitation about getting involved in a situation that had to do with drug addicts. I had known several families whose children had started using Crystal Meth, and watched chaos unfold: it was like living in a blender. Homes were broken into, cars and belongings stolen, lies and excuses and fighting and tears…it was a lot to take on, in addition to a newborn. I couldn't really blame them. And Dude's father was AWOL. That was probably not a good sign.

A few days later, Dude had a visit with his mom at CPS offices, and Sam came with me to town to drop him off. We spent the two hours of their visitation grocery shopping and running errands, then parked outside the CPS building to wait. When they brought Dude downstairs, the social worker stepped out of the elevator empty-handed, followed by Jess, who was carrying just the diaper bag. And walking right behind *her* was an angry looking man, holding Dude.

Sam and I both jumped out of the car.

We were introduced to Dude's dad. Matt was sullen, and looked at Sam as though he was trying to stare him down. It was uncomfortable, but Sam cheerfully stuck out his hand and introduced himself. "Matt? Hi, I'm Sam. Nice to meet you. Congratulations on your son!"

Matt relaxed slightly, but was not letting go of Dude. He muttered something and glared at me.

"Hi Matt." I smiled and tried not to look terrified.

"He wants to know what's wrong with his eye." Jess explained.

"Oh, well, we don't really know." I explained. "I took him to the doctor, and he has some ointment for it. It might just be a little cold, but instead of having a runny nose he has a runny eye!" I was trying to keep it light – real light. This man looked like he wanted to punch someone, and he definitely did not look like he wanted to hand over that baby.

"Okay!" the social worker cheerfully called. She had opened the door to the car. "Let's get baby out of the wind!" Matt reluctantly handed him over and I was relieved when the social worker escorted them both back inside and took them upstairs to her office while I fumbled with the buckles of the car seat.

"Was that guy at the pediatrician's?" Sam asked worriedly as we drove away.

"No. At least, I don't think so. I didn't know that anyone had heard from him since the birth."

The following Friday was Dude's two week checkup. We were seeing a different doctor because it was the week between Christmas and New Year's Eve, and the regular pediatrician was on vacation. I had been concerned that Jess AND Matt would show up, and I got there early so that I would be in the waiting room, where there was security and other people sitting around. I did not want to have to interact with them in the parking lot, and I dreaded trying to leave with the baby after the visit. But after all of my worry and precautions, no one showed up – which was probably a good thing. It turns out this pediatrician had been at the hospital for Dude's delivery, and she was still processing that experience. "Are they getting him back?" was her first question, asked in wide-eyed disbelief.

Apparently there had been quite a scene on the ward when Child Protective Services had arrived following notification of a positive drug test for mother and baby. "Who do I talk to about that?" the pediatrician looked up from her files. "I have some things I need to say." I learned a lot that day about how drugs interact with birth – according to the doctor, many times using crystal meth can actually bring on labor, which means that mothers arrive at the hospital right after doing the drugs, high and out of control, and scared witless. It makes it easy to identify drug-users, but it also means that the babies are born high as well, which can be a challenge.

"It was a total circus." The doctor informed me. "Crazy. Absolutely nuts."

I brought up the eye infection because the hospital had never called with the test results, and the doctor agreed that there was a good chance he had picked up the infection from his mother during birth. While the doctor checked his eyes, I brought up the fact that Dude's mom was really gung-ho about his circumcision - even though it made me feel slightly sick to my stomach to think that I might have to be there when it happened. But the doctor assured me that circumcising a preemie was the very least of their priorities.

I left the office feeling somewhat validated – the doctor believed me when I told her the mother had seemed high at the last appointment. "Of course she was!" the doctor exclaimed. "Not only is she a teenage drug user, but now her baby has been taken away, her body is changing, her milk is coming in, she has constant reminders that her baby is with someone else because she couldn't take care of him, she might be facing prosecution of some sort for possession or child endangerment, she is probably struggling with post-partum depression - why wouldn't she be using?"

As I drove home, I thought about this young mother. She was clearly struggling. She needed help, but talking to her when she was high wouldn't do any good at all. I hoped that she would be clean at our next visit. Maybe I could talk to her then. I wasn't a counselor or a social worker…..but I was a mom, and I wanted the best for her baby.

In the meantime, Dude was slowly waking up from his drug-induced haze. In the beginning, he had alternated between sleeping and screaming. His days and nights were all mixed up – which is common for newborns but really hard to deal with when the baby is inconsolable. And Dude was inconsolable. Maybe it was the drugs, maybe it was just his personality, but I would pace and rock and sing and talk and snuggle, sometimes lying on the floor next to his little vibrating chair comforting him while I tried to nap for a few minutes at a time. The only place he slept consistently was in the Baby Bjorn, so there were many nights that I reclined on the sofa with Dude sleeping soundly strapped to my chest. I learned to appreciate the quiet, and stop worrying so much about whether I actually slept or not. A good thing, because there was a whole lot of "not" in the first month or so.

The next week, I dropped Dude off for his two hour visit with Jess, at the CPS office. When I came back to pick him up, the social worker and his mom brought him downstairs together. Jess kissed him goodbye, handed him to me with a smile, and walked off checking her phone. As I buckled him in, I asked the social worker how the visit had gone. "It went okay," she said slowly.

"Can I ask you a question?" I straightened up and took the diaper bag that she was holding. "Does it seem weird to you that Dude's mom seems so casual about all of this? I mean, I don't want her to cry – but I think *I* would be crying if my baby was going home with someone else."

She leaned up against the car. "Well, just between you and me..........she wants to give him up. She doesn't want to get clean. She likes her lifestyle the way it is."

I closed my eyes for a moment. "Oh." I tucked a blanket over Dude's feet and shut the back door firmly.

"Nothing is going to happen right away," the social worker reassured me. "She is going to think about it. But she doesn't want to go to rehab. She gave up the spot they had for her."

"And none of her relatives will take him?"

The social worker shook her head slowly. "Nope." Her voice was flat. What was there to say, really. Here was a beautiful baby, with a huge family – and none of them would take him. It didn't make any sense to me. I waved to the worker and climbed into the car to drive home, adjusting my mirror so that I could keep an eye on the precious cargo sleeping in the backseat.

At Dude's one month checkup, I found myself once again at the clinic with his mom, sitting in the windowless waiting room for over an hour. I could tell right away that she was high, and my heart sank. She sat next to me, twitching and looking like she wanted to crawl out of her skin. Her eyes were in constant restless motion and she rocked back and forth clutching him to her chest awkwardly. At one point she turned to me and asked – almost in desperation – if I would adopt him. "I can't do this." She told me. "If I give him up will you be able to adopt him?" I sat forward and tried to hold her attention.

"You think you might give him up?" My mind was racing. I had no idea what to say. "What does your mom think?" I was trying to remain calm, but my inner voice was screaming in my ear: *Why wouldn't someone in her family take custody?* This was crazy.

"She said she would support me, whatever I decided."

I could barely look at her, my heart was just....breaking. She sat holding that precious baby, obviously struggling with something so much stronger than she was. This drug is so terrible. It changes people – sometimes forever. Maybe it was for the best, then. Maybe this was the very best thing she could do for him. I didn't know his father, didn't know what kind of situation she was in, and I certainly was in no position to judge her. So I took a deep breath, and started talking.

"There are so many families that want to adopt babies," I began. "And I love this little guy. But I think if you are going to give him up, that you should meet with a few families and be sure that you have found the right family for him. We are so fortunate to have two kids already – I would love to see someone else be given the opportunity to be a parent."

She glanced up at me. "You don't want him?"

"No, that's not it. That is not it at all." I was calm on the outside, but inside I was totally freaking out. Don't want him? Who wouldn't want him? "Listen. I would be happy to sit down with you and meet some families who are waiting to adopt. But the decision would be yours to make. You can choose an adoptive family for him. You have control over this entire situation."

She sat back against the pink vinyl seat and stared down at him. "No, I don't. He's a foster."

I leaned forward and caught her eye. "It's temporary, you know. If you get clean, and get a job and a place to live, you can get him back."

I didn't know if this was true. I had no idea what the legalities were, but I knew that she felt hopeless, and it seemed like a really terrible place to be. What would be her motivation to get clean?

She looked up at me. "I'm not ready. I can't do this."

Truth be told, I wasn't ready for this either. I had a new job and three kids and no childcare. I was struggling to adjust to parenting a newborn too.

The first stop every time I bring home a new foster baby is the WIC office. This organization provides nutritional support for pregnant and new mothers and their children. It covers the cost of formula, which means that I have to get each child signed up right away, or I am going to spend a fortune on feedings. But usually that is the biggest financial hurdle, and easily crossed. With this case I had a new complication – a job offer I had accepted before Dude had even been born. I found myself in the very strange position of needing a nanny for my foster child.

After a few phone calls, I discovered that there is an organization to help with that cost as well – but it is not nearly as easy to get signed up for benefits. This confused me – you would think that with a desperate need for foster parents, there would be a more streamlined way to get funds to cover childcare for a foster child – especially since placements come with less than 24 hours' notice. I didn't have time for a month of bureaucracy. But that is exactly what I got. I had to hire a sitter – because the baby was too young for day care – and the sitter had to be fingerprinted and background checked. They needed paystubs and letters from employers. It was insane. It didn't matter that the childcare was for a child in state custody – they needed our personal information. I was not happy. We are not wealthy – but we do not qualify for public assistance. I would love this baby like my own; do whatever he needed, buy the clothes and bottles and blankets and toys. But we just didn't have the budget to pay for a full time babysitter. I needed to work – and that money was supposed to be paying our bills, not paying for a babysitter for a two week old baby that showed up on a Sunday afternoon. Foster mothers do not get paid maternity leave. I needed childcare, and I couldn't afford it. Was this part of being a foster parent? I found that hard to believe. It was no wonder people weren't volunteering for the program.

I was assured time and again that it would just take a few weeks, and that we would be approved. But every time I handed them more paperwork or they asked for further documentation, the staffers in the office were obviously disgusted that I was requesting financial assistance. They made me feel as though I was taking advantage. I thought they needed to take a walk in my shoes and stop judging me.

It was a very uncomfortable situation, but there was no way around it. If I was going to be a foster parent and work, I had to jump through their hoops and disclose a lot of personal information in the hopes that somehow I might not go broke in the process.

Chapter 15 The Dude Abides

Dude was a scrappy little guy, and every time I told someone his story – the little of it I was allowed to disclose for privacy reasons – people always commented on how miraculous his very existence was; especially considering the fact that he was born the week before Christmas. It was a perfect Christmas miracle, people said time and again. I was in heaven - that was for sure. My mothering instinct had kicked in right away. I could sense when he was getting agitated, ready for sleep, hungry, or needing to be taken to a quiet area away from the holiday excitement.

I brought him with me everywhere, including work for the first few weeks, tucked away in his carrier or curled in my arms. I was exhausted, but as days passed and he continued to thrive I began to forget that he had such a hard start in life. The only time I was ever really concerned about him was when he didn't blink as I tried to wash his face.

It started when he had that eye infection at Christmas. It was a stubborn one that required two courses of antibiotic ointment. For several weeks, I would put the ointment on the end of my clean fingertip each morning and evening, and then put my finger in the corner of his eye and begin to draw it across the lid as the doctor had showed me. Dude never batted an eye. He never closed his eye in response to having something stuck in it, and that seemed strange.

191

And because he never closed his eye in response to having it wiped or prodded, I learned to start from the upper eyelid and encourage him to close his eye with gentle pressure, so that I could wipe it clean without touching his eyeball with the cloth. I started paying closer attention. He didn't look at me while he was being fed, but it wasn't just that he didn't look at *me* - he didn't look at anyone. No matter who held him or fed him, he stared off in the distance. When I talked to him he looked somewhere over my shoulder. When I bathed him in the tiny molded baby bathtub, he watched the wall.

If I spoke he would follow the sound, turning his head to look in my direction. My voice would calm him when he was upset, so I called to him from across the room or crooned as I rocked him in my arms. In bright sunlight he would squint and squirm and turn away, folding himself up into my armpit with his mittened fists pressed on either side of his forehead. That was something……wasn't it? So I continued to keep him near me, letting him squirm his way up under my chin or bury his face into my collarbone for comfort. But still, he didn't look *at* anything – at least, not anything that was shown to him or anyone who tried to engage with him. He didn't make eye contact, didn't track objects or watch the lights that flashed on his bouncy chair.

I held up toys and offered him his pacifier. I danced and jumped around, hoping he might turn in my direction. But he remained unfazed.

I waved my fingers in his face and jangled my keys. He never blinked.

Was this normal? I started calling friends with babies to ask questions like "Does your baby ever look at you? If you poke your baby in the face, does he close his eyes?"

The universal response began with "Um, I don't poke my baby in the face, actually."

Right.

Maybe I was being paranoid. I would ask the doctor at our next appointment.

But as I sat at the doctor's office that day with Dude's mom for his one month checkup, and she was asking me about adopting him and telling me she couldn't handle being a parent, it seemed like a bad time to be mentioning my concerns to the pediatrician in front of her. If she was overwhelmed at the thought of parenting, I was concerned that the idea of parenting a child with any sort of "issue" was going to push her right over the edge.

We got called in to the exam room just then, and as we waited for the doctor we talked a bit more. I encouraged her to think about her decision very carefully. Their Ohana Conference was coming up, and I reminded her that the conference was supposed to help her make a plan to get Dude back. She stared at me dully, clearly not believing it was possible. "Listen," I insisted, "if you want to keep him, they can help you do that. If you want to give him up for adoption, they can help you do *that* too. Just spend the next few weeks thinking about what YOU want, what you really, truly want deep down inside. Do you want to give him up? Or do you want to get him back? You are still in control of this situation. But no matter what you decide, his father is going to have to agree with you."

She stared at the floor, and I immediately felt terrible for having brought up Dude's father. Where was that guy, anyway?

The appointment went smoothly, Dude got an immunization and then we all started getting ready to leave while the doctor wrote in Dude's chart. I took a breath and brought up the blinking thing – trying to remain really casual about it: Hey Doc, I noticed he doesn't really blink. Is that normal?

The pediatrician paused in his note-taking. "What do you mean, he doesn't blink?"

"Well," I began, "he doesn't close his eyes. When I was putting the ointment in there like you showed me, he never closed his eyes – not even with my finger right in his face. But what really worries me is that he doesn't seem to track, either. He doesn't follow anything with his eyes, or look at anything specific. He just kind of stares off into space." Dude's mother stood there silently, staring down at her son. I could see her trying to catch his eye, trying to prove me wrong. The doctor walked over and poked his finger right in Dude's face. Dude stared at the ceiling. "Huh." The doctor said. "Well, he is still so young it's hard to tell if this is something to worry about…..but it is definitely possible that the drugs could have consequences we won't know about for years… cognitive, but also neurological. I'll send a note over to the therapists."

Dude's mother never said a word. When we left the clinic, she handed Dude over to me and I encouraged her, again, to think about what she really wanted for Dude. And that I would help her in any way I could. Everything was going to be okay. Really.

She looked relieved. "Okay, I'll think about it." She turned and climbed in her brother's battered sedan, and lit a cigarette as they drove away.

The pediatrician had referred us to an organization that offers various therapeutic assistance and parenting classes. When a foster child is referred to their program (and many foster children are) someone from the organization will come to our house and assess the child. They sit on the floor, helping infants to work on lifting their head, or crawling in the beginning. And as the kids get older the therapies evolve. Speech therapy, physical therapy,

It can take a while to get your first visit with a therapist. Just like everything else that relies on government monies, they are short-staffed and under-funded. When the day of our appointment finally arrived, I had been worried for quite some time. The nurse completed a thorough assessment and then we sat and talked about my concerns. She reassured me that it was still early days, and reminded me of his prematurity. His eye muscles may just be immature. And yes, the drugs could also be a factor. And he had that eye infection…. It could be nothing.

But I had to be sure. There was this feeling, this nagging little feeling in my chest. All of those drugs, maybe she was drinking too. Maybe he *did* have chlamydia. Maybe it was something else. Maybe it was nothing at all.

I needed to know. I couldn't leave it to time or chance – what if someone else got custody, or adopted him, and this just fell through the cracks? No, if there was something wrong I had to make sure it was noted, addressed, diagnosed, resolved……. I couldn't leave it for someone else to worry about, because who else *was* there? From that point on, every doctor, nurse, therapist, social worker, and experienced parent I met was handed the baby, and then asked for their personal assessment. I am sure most people thought I was over-reacting, but I was unwavering. And many people, once it was pointed out to them, agreed that he was not making any eye contact or following objects with his eyes. While most doctors want facts and test results and proof that something is wrong before pursuing a patient concern, pediatric specialists are a different breed. They have seen a mother's instinct at work and seeing me with my kids – foster, biological and adopted - assured them that the mothering instinct does not require a biological connection between mother and child. And so I was persistent. I had to follow up. I had to follow through. I had to wait, impatiently, for the next appointment, the next assessment, I just kept telling them, over and over again, anyone who would listen. Something was not right.

We waited together, he and I. Asleep and awake, moving through the dark and the light in three hour intervals, and it was then, when I was most worried, and watching his every response, that I began to struggle with the reality - that this was all just a temporary arrangement. He needed someone to be there for him, and I worried that if he was transferred out of my care, that this might not get the attention it deserved. And my heart began to break, just a little bit more every day.

When the social worker came to pick Dude up for his next visit, I told her that his mom had brought up adoption to me. She shook her head sadly and we talked for a few minutes about the Ohana Conference. I told her that I had decided not to attend, so that the families would have some privacy to discuss their options. I also brought up my concerns about his vision, and she agreed: she noticed it too.

"When my grandson was born," she confided, "he looked right at me. He stared at me like he was memorizing my face! This one doesn't do that." I buckled him in to the car, and she took notes - it was important to get this checked out.

"I'm going to make an appointment with a specialist." I told her as I closed the car door. "I want to get to the bottom of this."

It turns out all of my worry was for naught. While we were waiting the few weeks between making the appointment and actually seeing the specialist, Dude started watching me from time to time. At first, it was just for a few seconds, and then he began watching me while I fed him. We bought him a new toy that he absolutely loved, and he reached for it one day out of the blue. I felt like he had just competed in the Olympics.

In the meantime, his family had their Ohana Conference, and Jess had announced that she wanted to get clean and raise her son. I got the news during yet another hand-off to the social worker before a visit. "She's going into rehab." the worker informed me. "She wants to get him back. Things are moving in the right direction."

After they drove away, I came back inside and sat down on the couch to get my head around it. He was going back to his mom. Things were moving in the right direction.

"I sure hope so." I thought.

Once his mother agreed to go into rehab, she had to wait for a spot in the program. I cannot say for certain if she was still using at this time, but I can say this: once Jess got through the initial detox, and was transferred to a halfway house specifically for mothers who are recovering addicts, she was like a new person.

Now sober, she knew who I was, but she did not recognize my children, something we discovered when she came out to get the baby from my car and, upon seeing my son in the passenger seat – a kid she had met several times and spent countless hours with waiting for doctor's appointments – she turned and asked me "Is that your boy?" When I replied in the affirmative she smiled and waved. "HI! I'm Jess!"

"Um, nice to meet you?" he replied. As we drove away he turned to me, incredulously. "She doesn't *remember me*?"

"No, sweetie," I said, ruffling his hair. "She doesn't remember much of anything from when Dude was new."

"That is crazy." He muttered as he turned back to his video game.

The following week, Jess came bouncing out the front door wearing a new outfit and makeup – it was the first time I had ever seen her take any real care with her appearance. "Hey!" I greeted her with a grin. "You look great!"

"I'm got my hair cut!" she grinned. "And I'm wearing makeup!"

"I can see that! It's great." I gave her a hug and headed off with a wave.

And as Jess slowly came out of her fog of drug use, I watched her become a loving mother to Dude. It was hard for her to play catch up, and I wasn't sure how much support she was getting from her family.

She kept asking me to leave "his carseat" and I finally asked the social worker why Jess did not have a carseat of her own for Dude. "I mean, she thought she was bringing him home from the hospital, right? She didn't know the state was going to take him. Her mother has carseats for her kids, so they use them. There must be a carseat somewhere." But apparently there was no carseat to be found. I don't know if Jess sold it for drugs, or if it was returned to the store when the baby was taken from her, or if it was just abandoned at the hospital. All I knew was, she couldn't have my carseat. I reminded the social worker that Jess may not have any idea what she needed for Dude, and that maybe it would be helpful to give her a checklist, like the one every other new mother seemed to have, of the things she needed: carseat, crib, diapers, wipes, clothes, diaper bag…if she had nothing, she needed a list of some kind so that she could refer to it while preparing to regain custody. The judge would want to see that she was being proactive.

The issue I was running into was that the state, and the halfway house, and the people around her, were not really preparing Jess for parenting. Maybe in theory they were giving her some useful information and support while she got clean – but she needed real-world, real-time encouragement and assistance. For example – did she know how to apply for WIC, state health insurance, housing assistance and food stamps? She was going to need those things while she got on her feet after rehab. And what about teaching her to watch for cues that her baby would give her? Did she know what to do if he began to cry? Did she have the inner dialogue telling her to check his diaper, figure out if he was hungry or tired? Did she know that she needed to watch for signs that he was teething or not feeling well? Did she even know what signs to watch for? Because she had never cared for him for more than a few supervised hours, I was concerned. I didn't want her to be set up for failure. I believed that she could do this – but she needed guidance and support, and she needed to learn to trust her instincts, which had been numbed by drug use and time away from her baby.

The first hint of a maternal instinct came one afternoon when I came to pick Dude up from the halfway house. "He feels warm, to me." Jess said hesitantly. "Do you think he's getting sick?" I felt his head, his neck, his belly, and agreed with her.

"He does feel warm, do you have a thermometer?"

She looked downcast. "No, I don't have one of those."

I looked around the halfway house – a place that's entire mission statement was to help women - former drug addicts with no resources of their own - become mothers, and wondered what, exactly, they were doing to meet that goal. If she showed any instinct or concern for her child at all, why wasn't it being addressed – never mind encouraged? Did they really not have a thermometer in this entire facility? I felt this flash of anger, but just as with everything else connected to "the system" I realized that there wasn't much point in that. "I'll call the pediatrician and let you know what they say" I promised her.

It turned out that while, yes, he did have a fever, he didn't have an ear infection or a cold, and we chalked it up to new teeth coming it. I bought Jess a bottle of Tylenol to keep with her in case she ever needed it, and encouraged her to track down a thermometer the next time she was concerned about a fever. "If you ever, ever feel like something is wrong with him, I want you to go find one of the parenting instructors and ask for help, okay?"

She nodded, relieved that her concerns had been addressed. "Okay, I will. When is his next checkup? Matt wants to come too."

I gave her a tight smile. Fabulous.

We were on track for reunification – it would happen in the next few months, and Dude would start spending the night, one night a week, at the halfway house. Another night would be added every week and then he would transition over to her care full time. While I was relieved that they were giving Jess time to get used to the idea of parenting, I had to admit that living in a halfway house with a daycare on premises and classes all day long was not really going to prepare her for living on her own, working full time, and raising a toddler. In the facility, there was always another mom to hold Dude, or help her make dinner, and she never had to worry about paying the bills, or getting up and going to work after being awake all night with a fussy baby. I know how stressful parenting can be, and I was always worried that the stress might lead her back to drugs if she didn't have the education and support she needed.

The first step, I thought, would be making sure she had a great pediatrician. We switched Dude from the free clinic to an actual pediatric practice, with a doctor I knew and respected. More importantly, it was a doctor that neither parent had ever met before. There would be no history, no judgment, and no anxiety: a fresh start for everyone. I gave the pediatrician a little background – just enough to be aware during their visits, and keep an eye out for anything that seemed cause for concern. I reassured Jess that the new doctor was fantastic and that the new office was a better choice – they had multiple locations so that no matter where she lived, an office would be close by. They had an after-hours clinic so that if she had a concern during the evening she could bring him in to be seen right away. I wanted to set her up for success, and I felt like finding her a great pediatrician was an important part of that.

A few weeks later, I met Jess and Matt at the doctor's office. They were both clean and dressed nicely, smelling of soap instead of the usual cigarettes. I was relieved to see them passing the baby back and forth, smiling at him and at each other. They looked like a happy little family. As we sat and waited our turn, Jess pulled a gallon size plastic bag of sour candies out of her diaper bag. I checked my watch. It was 8:35am. I tried not to look appalled.

During the exam, the doctor asked them some questions, and asked if they had any questions for her. They both shook their heads silently. Dude was wiggling around in Matt's lap. "He might be hungry." I told Matt, who was trying to hang on to his son while he twisted and arched his back. "He didn't finish his bottle this morning." I handed Matt the rest of the bottle from my cooler, and Matt gave me a look of disgust, handing it back to me and asking Jess for a bottle that wasn't so cold.

I was bemused. To have a parent who has lost custody of their child criticize me for giving that child a cold bottle was insulting and hysterical all at the same time. As much as I wanted to lecture him about priorities and about how formula will go bad if it isn't refrigerated, I held my tongue. Things were going well. I did not want to say or do anything that might upset anyone in the room – but most of all I did *not* want to upset Matt. I didn't know anything about him other than his name. I didn't know whether he was using drugs, or had anger issues, I didn't know if he had any other kids or a police record. All I knew was that he wanted his baby, and his baby lived with me. I did not want to be seen as his opponent – I wanted to be supportive.

At the end of the visit, I left Dude with Jess and Matt for a few hours of visitation. They were going to fill his prescription and the doctor had encouraged them to buy a few staples to have in their diaper bag – ointment, Tylenol….that sort of thing. They didn't seem to have any idea what they should put in there besides diapers and candy. As we parted ways outside the pharmacy in the lobby, Jess pulled me aside and quietly asked if they were going to have to pay for "that other stuff".

"The Tylenol and ointment? Well, yes. Don't either one of you have any money?"

She shook her head and looked at me, as though I should volunteer to pay. I just smiled and said "Well, buy as much of it as you can today, you have time to get these things slowly over the next few weeks."

"Okay, thanks." She turned back to her baby, and his father. Her family. I walked out to my car and sat for a moment. Then I turned on the engine and drove home, the empty carseat in the back visible in my rearview mirror.

Chapter 16 Saying Goodbye

The last few months that Dude was in our custody was a time of wildly shifting emotions. Every two weeks, Dude added another night to his stay at the halfway house with his mother. And so, over the course of that last month he spent less time with us, and more time with his mom. When we had shifted to having him three nights a week compared to his mother's four nights, I started wondering why this made sense. What was the point in my bringing him back to my home for just two nights of the week? For one night? My house was still full of toys and his bassinet was next to my bed. The stroller was taking up precious space in my trunk and his carseat, when it wasn't strapped in the backseat, was sitting in the middle of my living room – a constant reminder that he was leaving, but not quite gone.

It was a strange existence. We had an infant, with all of the infant trappings - part of the time. I was still completely beholden to the State of Hawaii - part of the time. I needed reliable childcare – one day a week. We still couldn't go on vacation. We still couldn't wash all the baby clothes and pack them away. And all of the things that needed to be done like doctor's appointments, WIC visits for formula, and buying new clothes for a rapidly growing baby still had to happen – in a smaller and smaller window of time.

But soon, I knew, that time would come to an end altogether. And I was trying to prepare all of us for the day when everything would be "back to normal". Only, in my head, I felt like "normal" really meant "missing a huge important piece." The stuff that was strewn all over our house would be put back in storage, and the bottles would disappear from my precious counter space, and I could get out of bed in the middle of the night without worrying about waking the baby because I accidentally bumped the bassinet in the dark. Life was going to be so much easier, I kept telling myself. It was the only way to get through the day sometimes. To keep myself from getting emotional every week when I handed him over to his mother for longer and longer periods of time, I tried to stay busy in his absence.

My first order of business was planning a party. As the summer approached, and as people saw me without Dude more and more often, we started getting a lot of questions about how this whole reunification thing worked. What the plan was. People worried that his mother might change her mind, or that he might somehow end up back in the system. People worried that he had already gone back to his mother full-time: they wanted to see him before he was reunited with his mother permanently. I wanted to give everyone in our community – the babysitters and bottle washers, the friends and family - an opportunity to say goodbye and have some closure. I realized that all of us loved and cared for him, and that I would not be the only one wondering how he was doing when his birthday rolled around or when The Big Lebowski was on cable late at night, with the hapless "Dude" played by Jeff Daniels. I felt like it was only fair to let everyone see him, take a picture with him, give him one last cuddle……

My brother designed the invitation, inserting a photo of Dude into a screenshot of Jeff Daniels, John Goodman and Steve Buscemi at a bowling alley in a scene from "The Big Lebowski".

I planned the food, and carefully scheduled the party for the last weekend night that Dude would be at our house – then I invited everyone who had spent time with him to come over. Seeing that date on the calendar was difficult some times…..it felt real, and it felt soon. Too soon.

A few days before the party, the phone rang and I saw the now-ominous "Hawaii State Gov" on the screen. I didn't think much of it, but when I was informed that his reunification was being accelerated, and I would not have him on the night of the party, I was bewildered. Taking a breath, I explained that we were having his going away party that night. The social worker seemed confused.

"You're having a party for him?"

To her credit, she immediately switched the visitation schedule back, and the party went on as planned – but it was a last reminder that this was not my baby, and that ultimately I was going to have to let go.

At least, I thought it was the last reminder.

In no time at all, we were down to the last two weeks. Dude was going to spend 1 night a week with us for two weeks, and then would be permanently transitioned to his mother. It seemed ridiculous. One night? I just didn't see the benefit, but I tried to remind myself that it was another way they encouraged his mother to stay in the program – she had to earn full custody back week by week.

So for those last two Wednesdays, I arranged to take time off of work, and spend them with all three kids. I wanted to be there to help them through the transition and I didn't see any point in having Dude for 24 hours and having six of those hours spent with a babysitter.

And then, on Tuesday morning – the last day that I would be picking Dude up – the social worker called and the "Hawaii State Gov" flashed on my screen. I answered cheerfully, hoping that this was just a "let's wrap this up" call with my checklist of things to bring with him when he went back to his mother the next day, forever.

Instead, I was informed that I did not need to pick up Dude. That he would not be spending that last night with us. And I sat down on the couch, stunned.

I didn't get to say goodbye? After seven months, I didn't even get to give him a kiss?

This was unthinkable. How – why – would anyone think that this was okay? Was our commitment so easily dismissed? Were my children really not allowed to say goodbye one last time? I wouldn't be able to give his mom a hug and tell her how proud I was of her?

I was never going to see him again. The answers to my questions were curt. When I brought up my own kids, and getting an opportunity for some closure, I was told – reluctantly – that perhaps a visit could be arranged so that we could see him, if I felt it was really necessary.

And right then, I got angry. I found my limit in that moment. I saw the very edge of decency and fairness and I realized that to them, this case was just a file and would always be that – names and numbers on a page amongst many pages in a file amidst many files. Our relationship and commitment was not important, as long as the baby showed up for visitation. And as soon as they didn't need us anymore, we should close the file just like they did. Case closed.

I cried, then. I cried for Dude. I cried selfishly for myself. I cried as I packed up his diapers and formula and clothes and toys and the gifts he had received at his party. I cried as I drove to the halfway house hoping for a last chance to see Dude, and was met at the door by a staffer, my packages taken from me with an emotionless thank you. I was dismissed from his life like an employee being fired abruptly.

And that was that. The security door closed and latched in my face.

I was numb for a while. I spent that last day off – the one I had planned to spend cuddling Dude – washing and packing up the bassinet and carseat. Sam came home and helped me get it all up in the attic. Within a few hours, it was as though the last six months had been completely erased.

When people heard the story they had strong reactions. No one shrugged their shoulders and said "Well, what do you expect?" or

"You knew it was coming." It seemed inhumane, the way the ties were severed. I certainly felt as though he had been removed from my life with a surgical precision. I was, I think, in a daze for the first week. I slept a lot. I packed up our bags and flew to New England for a month with the kids. And even there, thanks to Facebook, everyone knew what had happened and that I was, in a way, grieving. They passed me babies to cuddle, and slowly I was able to let it go. I was able to remember how it felt. That it was like this every time. It's like giving birth – you develop a sort of selective amnesia about the process, remembering the beautiful parts and forgetting the rest. If you didn't you would probably never do it again.

Chapter 17: Another Child, Not My Own

It took a while to get over Dude, as you might expect. It was not the heartbreak of never seeing him again, but the anger I felt at social workers who treated my family – and I assume many others - as disposable. I felt used, and insignificant. Unappreciated by the very system that I wanted so much to contribute to, I just wasn't sure I could continue to participate in a program that was clearly not working in a thoughtful and comprehensive way.

For a while, we just sat in a holding pattern: available, technically…..but not really available. When a worker called with a case I found excuses. I wasn't ready, or we had something going on that would make it difficult to take custody at a moment's notice. One day we got a call two weeks before I chaired the school's annual fundraiser – a festival that I had been planning for months. There was no way I could pull it off wearing a Baby Bjorn, with a few hours of sleep under my belt. So for nine months we were "baby-less". And then, just like an expectant mother, at the nine month mark I suddenly felt ready. The universe was picking up what I was laying down: a series of events brought us two babies in as many weeks.

On a Thursday afternoon, the very same day that we were celebrating Lucy's birth eight years prior, another baby was being born. He was delivered at the same hospital she had been, but that is where the similarities ended. He was born high on crystal meth, and Child

Protective Services was called. On Friday, as we were loading up Lucy's friends in the car for a sleepover, my phone rang.

Because my phone battery is always almost dead by dinnertime, it was plugged into the car charger and connected to the console by a short cord. To answer it, Sam needed to bend forward with his forehead practically touching the dashboard. And because he is not 100% sure how to use my "fancy" touch screen phone (he still held out against technology, agreeing only to use a clamshell-style flip phone from 1998) he tends to press the screen a few times and then just sort of shout at it.

So there he was, bent double in the front seat, shouting into a phone that was attached to the console by a wire about 6" long. Luckily he had managed to turn on the speakerphone during the course of his attempt to answer the call, so I could hear everything that was going on as I drove.

It was our social worker, and he was calling to make sure we were home, because he had a baby for us. A baby boy.

Because at that moment we were about to host a sleepover, I didn't have a lot of time to chat, but Sam was peppering the worker with questions, and saying things like "Well, we have a lot going on and might not be able to-"
"Just ask him when I need to be ready."

213

Sam looked at me, and shook his head. But I was confident. Defiant, even. It was a sign – a baby born on Lucy's birthday? No brainer. That baby needed me, and I was starting to think that I might need him. Yes, we would take the baby. Yes, we knew the social worker who would be calling us over the weekend. Yes, of course. Yes, no problem. Yes, absolutely. The worker said goodbye and without even looking at Sam, I said "It's fine. Hang up the phone."

He looked over his shoulder at the six girls shrieking and giggling in the back of the Suburban we had rented for the weekend. And he shook his head and sighed, and started pressing on the touch screen trying to hang up the call.

Friday night passed in a whirlwind of top 40 sing-alongs, ice cream sundaes and late night whispers. In the morning the girls were collected by their parents, and headed home exhausted and strung out on bacon and red velvet treats. Saturday afternoon we took Lucy to lunch and bought her a few gifts, and I had pretty much forgotten that we were waiting for a phone call. But as we headed home the phone rang again. The social worker was heading to the hospital, were we ready? I got some basic information about the case, and then asked the most important question on my mind at the moment: Did I have time to go to Costco? Because chances were very good that I wasn't going to get there again for a while.

The baby arrived on Saturday afternoon, just before dinner, and about 24 hours after the first call. He was dropped off with a diaper bag, new and fully stocked with everything he would need. Clean clothes, bottles, burp clothes, blankets, wipes, diaper rash cream – even antibiotic ointment and a jar of Vaseline. I was confused. This baby was obviously much anticipated, and his mother had taken great care to make sure she had everything she would need. How was it that she was using drugs? Drug addicts – crystal meth users in particular – are not known for their organization skills and accountability. And yet here was evidence that she took the arrival of her child seriously – at least seriously enough to prepare and spend money on things for the baby - instead of on drugs. She had clearly gone down a checklist and bought everything on it. The bag was neatly arranged, the clothes washed and folded. The plastic wipe container was full of wipes.

The social worker saw my confusion. "I don't think he'll be here for long," she assured me. "His mom wants him back. She is going to rehab on Monday morning. Oh man, she *really* cried when I left." I took him in my arms, swaddled in a huge fuzzy blanket even though it was about 80 degrees outside. I couldn't tell if his face was bright red because he was a newborn, or because he was so overdressed. I unwrapped him and got a good look.
Leo.

He was tiny and sleeping peacefully. We passed him around, took a bunch of photos, and then set him down in the bassinet. I finished unpacking the diaper bag and got everything put away. I was still wondering what the tube of Vaseline was for. In this day and age, it wasn't a diaper bag staple. When I changed his diaper, I realized why it was in there.

Leo had just been circumcised.

Because we chose not to circumcise Max, I had never seen a "fresh" circumcision before. Poor Leo cried as I wiped him off during that first change. I hastily smeared Vaseline over the end of his penis which looked really raw and sore. It was very unsettling. Was I hurting him? Doing something wrong? Or was he just crying because he was cold? I was happy when I had him dressed again and could take him over to the rocking chair and soothe him back to sleep. Poor little guy. I was shaken. This was the first time in a long time that something had happened with a foster baby, and I hadn't known what to do. After a few more equally upsetting diaper changes, I went online and researched "circumcision care". One site recommended I not use a baby wipe on a new circumcision until it was healed, so I stopped using the wipes and after that diaper changes were a lot easier. Lesson learned, unfortunately the hard way. After that experience, the rest of the week was very mellow. Holding a sleeping baby is one of the most peaceful ways to pass the time - even those moments during 2am feedings when I was blurry with sleep were sweet.

While we were busy loving and caring for Leo, a few miles away his mom was working hard to regain custody. She got herself into rehab, and followed every directive issued by child protective services. She had obviously prepared carefully for Leo's arrival – judging by the diaper bag alone I was sure that whatever had happened right before his birth, she knew right from wrong, and was doing everything she could to get back on the right track. It felt good to know she wanted him, and wanted to get clean for him. I didn't understand how she had made such a terrible decision to use drugs during her pregnancy, but it was clear she realized the enormity of her mistake, and wanted to make significant changes going forward. It was the ideal situation for my first case back - I really felt like I was doing something good, and helping a mom who needed – and wanted – the help. But then I saw her sitting outside the social worker's office, looking sullen, smoking a cigarette. It didn't match the vision I had in my head of the young mom eager to regain custody. I was nervous about interacting with her, so I circled the block and waited for her to leave. Drug users are unpredictable in general – and when a baby is involved it is easy for the relationships with the foster parents to be tenuous at best. I did not want a confrontation, and I was relieved to avoid one.

The following week I brought Leo to the rehab, and met his mother face to face for the first time. When I arrived I greeted the woman at the front desk with a big hug, like the strange family that we have become, taking care of these mothers and their children. I was nervous, but she reassured me that Leo's mom was anxious to meet me. The rehab is a fairly safe place, filled with mothers and children, healing and growing together – I had decided that I was comfortable enough to meet her here, and now I was so glad that I made that decision. Leo's mother came running down the hall and swept him up out of my arms, crying and kissing him and looking him over. Suddenly she stopped and looked up.

"Thank you." The tears were rolling down her cheeks and falling on his face. "Can I give you a hug?"

I was a little taken aback – sometimes birth mothers are not able to express their thanks this early in recovery – the wound from having their child taken from them too fresh in their minds, and everyone associated with that loss viewed suspiciously. But she shifted Leo over to the crook of one arm, and wrapped her other arm around me, squeezing tightly and thanking me again for taking such good care of him. I hugged her back, we talked for a moment about how sweet he was, and then she went off to the kitchen, and I went to get my hair cut. It was an appointment made weeks before Leo was even born - one of the many little details you don't think about when saying yes to a foster placement - and I was relieved that Leo's visitation with his mom coincided with my long-anticipated appointment time.

While I sat under the dryer I felt my phone vibrate, and I looked down at the screen. It was Leo's social worker. The call went to voicemail before I could answer it – and that was probably a good thing, because I have no idea how I would have responded had I actually taken that call.

The message was short and sweet. "Thank you for all you do, Leo is going to stay with his mother at rehab. You don't need to go back and pick him up today."

They did it again.

Chapter 18 The Revolving Door

Leo's abrupt departure was on a Tuesday. On Friday Sam and I were cleaning up, starting to put away all of the baby stuff that was once again scattered all over the house. I gave the bassinet to a friend who was expecting the birth of her own baby in a few weeks, along with the car seat and stroller and a few other things. But that night, as we were making our bed, I looked up at Sam and confessed something that had been nagging at me all week, and had prevented me from putting all of the baby gear away in the attic quite yet.

When Leo was returned to his mother, I felt as though the rug had been pulled out from under me - which is bizarre considering that I knew he would only be with us for a short while. But there I was, feeling this strange sense of "something is not right" when of course Leo being reunited with his mother was absolutely right, and heartwarming to be a part of. And since I was so confident that I played a part in strengthening a family – which is, after all, why we foster to begin with - I could not figure out why I felt so bereft. There was this nagging, keening feeling. A nameless, wordless thing tapping me on the shoulder. And then, out of the blue, it clicked.

Sam and I were securing the fitted sheet when I stopped - hit with this sudden knowledge, the answer to my confusion and feeling of loss. I sat up on the corner of the bed where I had been huddled wrestling with the last corner of the mattress.

"I'm not done."

"What?" he said absentmindedly, as he shook a pillow into the case.

"There's another baby. I'm telling you, that wasn't it. Leo was NOT it. There's something else going on."

Sam shook his head and rolled his eyes and went back to his pillow cases. I returned to the sheet, but I had a sudden feeling of peace and clarity. I decided to leave the crib up in the living room. And the next day, the very next day, my phone rang. There was an infant in the maternity ward needing placement, was I interested? No other information, just "could I take a newborn". I had only one question: "When?" Right away - in an hour or two. I said yes, and then walked inside to tell Sam I had manifested another baby.

He put his face in his hands, and rubbed his cheeks hard, and then grinned. "How the hell do you do that?"

"I don't know, I just *know*."

"It's incredible. I wish you could do that in Vegas."

I drove to the hospital and called upstairs. The social worker sounded almost giddy. "Seven pounds, eight ounces, she is beautiful and I'm just filling out the paperwork." When they appeared downstairs a while later, I peeked through the bundle of pink: "Beautiful" was a reach, but as I peered down at her she stretched a small, delicate hand with impossibly long fingers out of the sea of flannel, as if to say "How do you do?" Evie was a charmer, right from the start, and I fell very, very hard for that little hand with its peeling skin and translucent nails.

Her mother had not been as prepared as Leo's mother. In fact, she was not prepared at all. There was some question as to whether she even knew she was pregnant. Arriving at the hospital in a tee shirt and shorts, there was no carefully packed diaper bag, no freshly washed and folded clothes. The nurses in the maternity ward had worked together to find Evie a clean outfit and a blanket to go home, but other than what they dressed her in, she had nothing. And while I had a small stash of girl clothes from when Lucy was a baby, there was a lot I didn't have. So in her first few days, as word spread that we had a new foster baby and needed some girl clothes, Evie was showered with gifts from our family and friends - celebrated and welcomed into the world like most babies are. While her future was uncertain, for now she had the stability that she – and all newborns – deserved.

Evie and I understood one another. We spent long hours lying on the bed face to face, staring into each other's eyes. Sam and Max were equally enamored, and Lucy strutted around in the role of big sister to a little sister that she had long hoped for. We were just as giddy as if she had joined our family forever. While of course, I knew that this was foster care - that we were caring for someone else's baby, and that she would only be here for a while - the timeline seemed........fuzzy. This situation was different than past cases: there was no plan for her mother to go to rehab, no father had been identified, and her mother had left the hospital shortly after giving birth, when she learned that the baby was being placed in protective custody. Not wanting to interact with the police who would be arriving to file a report, she just put on her clothes and walked out the door.

And so I did the very worst thing I could do. I put all of that out of my mind and focused on this tiny, pink, squalling creature with long legs and thick brown hair. I held her and whispered to her that she was going to be just fine. I told her that we loved her, sang her songs about wild horses and moonlight, reassured her that this diaper change was going to be fast and the baby wipe wouldn't be so cold – which was a total lie, and she called me on it. She suffered no fools, this little one.

We went through the first 24 hours of sleepy sweetness, and then the next three days were a blur of endless crying and projectile vomiting and diarrhea, as Evie purged herself of all that she had been exposed to in utero. And then, after one final Exorcist-worthy puke-fest, she fell asleep with her head pressed up under my chin. She was peaceful from that moment forward.

And just as soon as we made it out of the dark woods of Evie's withdrawal, her mother turned up.

I felt almost sick to my stomach when I dropped her off with the social worker for that first visit. I called feeding instructions after them weakly as they walked away, and then I got back in the car and took a deep breath.

This is not your baby. This is not your baby. This baby is someone else's baby. This baby is going to see her mother. You are not her mother.

Silently, I repeated this to myself as I drove across town. I was close, dangerously close, to crying. I went to my happy place, searching for solace in the only way I knew how without a Target or TJ Maxx nearby: Goodwill.

I walked through Goodwill, and stopped at the bin of baby clothes. There, right on top, was a pair of jeggings. I love jeggings. I can't explain it, but they make me smile.

It was a sign. It had to be a sign. How the hell could a brand new pair of newborn jeggings be sitting there in Goodwill for any other reason? WHAT OTHER REASON COULD THERE POSSIBLY BE FOR THIS?

I bought the jeggings. And a dozen other things. And then Evie's visitation was over and I went back and stood outside and tried not to snatch her away from the worker who brought her out to me. I focused on staying calm and cool. I did everything I could to be chipper and friendly, tried to walk slowly back to the car, chatting with the social worker all the while instead of sprinting like I wanted to. "Keep it light," I told myself. "Don't let them know you care too much."

And then I buckled her into her carseat, kissed her sweet head and her impossibly soft cheeks, and gently closed the door to drive home.

Lucy greeted us as soon as I pulled into the driveway, busily digging through the bag of clothes I had bought that morning, until she came across the jeggings. She squealed with delight and raced off to put them in the washing machine so that Evie could wear them the next day. I got Evie out of the carseat and handed her to Sam, who was waiting with open arms.

That moment in the parking lot of CPS had been a moment of clarity: I was in trouble. I could play it cool, but I knew in my heart that I had gone too far. I had cared too much. The boundary had been crossed, and I was no longer thinking as a professional – it had gotten very personal for me in just a few short days. But there was nothing to be done about that. I had to just love her and not look ahead to the future. Stay in the present, and enjoy every moment I was given. But I knew: this one? She was going to break my heart, and there was nothing I could do about it. I had ignored the golden rule of foster parenting: You cannot forget - not for a moment - that you are caring for someone else's child.

Lucy came running back down the stairs, begging for a pair of jeggings so that she and Evie could match.

What could I say? Giving Evie back may be the very last thing I could do, the very hardest thing our family would ever experience. But there was no time to dwell on it: I had to find a pair of matching jeggings by tomorrow morning. Based on our recent experiences I knew full well - by tomorrow night, Evie could be gone.

Chapter 19 – And I am Telling You, She's Not Going.

It was unavoidable: From the moment I set eyes on Evie, I absolutely abandoned all common sense and reason, and broke every single rule of mine - and of the system in general - when it comes to foster parenting. I made it personal. I was not babysitting. I couldn't have cared less about her biological family. And now I was afraid that I had passed the point of no return.

I love all of the children we have cared for, each in their own way. I happily nurture them and guide them, and then I give them back to their mothers and I get on with life. But so help me, I could not imagine this little girl with anyone else but me as her mother.

This was very, very bad. For many reasons. The biggest reason is that she was not mine – she had a mother. Her mother may have been unpredictable and inconsistent, but still: Evie *did* have a mother and other relatives in the area. And within the foster care system the state will try everything they can to reunify the biological family, because that is absolutely the guiding principle of foster care: to provide biological parents and their relatives with resources and support and education, in the hope that they will be able to raise the child themselves. The foster system is not set up as an adoption agency - everyone involved in foster care knows that reunification is the goal. Social workers spend long, hard hours trying to assist the biological parents, while keeping their children safe.

I have always been very supportive of reunification. I have encouraged biological families time and again as they have tried to get their lives together, because I truly believe that a baby is the very best reason to get your life back on track……but not this time. Every time the social worker called to arrange a visitation with relatives, my jaw tightened and my heart pounded. And finally, after five days of this torture I had to say it out loud: "I don't support reunification in this case." As soon as the words came out, I was relieved. I knew that as a foster parent, this opinion was counter-productive. It is a huge conflict of interest. Absolutely inappropriate. Way, way out of line.

But it was the truth. I felt sick about it. I have heard that line "the heart wants what the heart wants" and I always thought it was a big bunch of baloney - an excuse for doing whatever the heck you felt like doing without concern for other people, for consequences, for right and wrong. And yet, here I was.

I have been caring for other people's children, in one way or another, since I was 9 years old. I am very good at keeping it professional, at remembering who the mother is, at not getting attached. And now I found myself at odds with everything I have ever known, everything I have ever believed about myself.

And I beat myself up about it, day after day. These feelings of protectiveness and belonging that I couldn't deny, even though I knew they were – at best – going to make the end of this case very difficult. I would lie awake at night as my mind raced. *I used to be good at this.*

Something has changed. Maybe I just have to stop. The fact is, you cannot be a foster parent if you are emotionally devastated at the end of every case. It's not good for anyone, and it makes it so much harder on the social workers, the foster children, and your own family and friends.

That is why I had decided to be honest with the social worker. I went so far as to suggest that they take me off the case entirely, and transfer Evie out of my home. But of course I didn't want them to do that. I wanted to have her with me as long as I possibly could, until the very last moment.

So Evie stayed with us, and I put on a brave face and tried to sound cheerful and rational. But in private, I cried.

I cried on the phone, I cried in the rocking chair late at night, I cried in the car driving her to visitations. I cried because I couldn't imagine keeping her any longer and because I didn't want to see her go. I cried because, knowing I wouldn't be a part of her future, I could only imagine the life she might have. I cried for her mother, I cried for the women who want to be mothers.

I cried at poop on the couch and puke in the car seat.

I cried because after two weeks Evie's bellybutton stump wouldn't come off and she really needed a bath (see poop and puke, above).

I cried when her mother didn't show up for visits, my heart aching for this little girl who I could not protect from her mother's neglect.

I cried when her mother *did* show up for visits, when Evie was returned to me with her diaper hanging off of her because it hadn't been put on correctly, or with two empty bottles which signified that she had been overfed during her one hour visit, because feeding her was the only way her mother knew to soothe her.

I wondered if it was possible to have postpartum mood swings when I was not only NOT postpartum, but post-menopausal?

(The answer to that is no.)

I felt like I was losing my mind. I didn't know what to do. I was at a loss at the prospect of losing her. And yet she was never mine to begin with.

Chapter 20 – The Baby I Left Behind

Summer was fast approaching, and with it our annual trip to New England. From the moment I took custody of Evie, everyone had known that there was a date: a date when I would be leaving the island for two months. And the question hung there, an elephant in every room during every conversation. Would I be allowed to bring her with me? I wanted to. And in the beginning, as her mother missed visit after visit and made it clear that she was nowhere near ready to parent, her guardian and social worker seemed to think it might actually happen. But finally, two weeks before we were set to leave, a new social worker was assigned. We had never met – and did not meet at any time during this case. The first email I received from her said – in no uncertain terms – that I would not be allowed to take the baby off island. Her grandmother wanted custody, and Evie would be living with her as soon as the licensing process was completed. I comforted myself with the knowledge that she would be with her grandmother on a different island, and hoped that the distance from her mother (and all of her myriad issues) would allow Evie to have the childhood she deserved. More than anything, I wanted Evie to have a family. I didn't want her to bounce from foster home to foster home. I didn't want her to be the kid who didn't know who her father was, or the kid whose mom lived on the streets. More than anything, I wished for normalcy for her. Being with her grandmother seemed like a step in the right direction.

So began the process of saying goodbye. I was grateful for the opportunity to prepare myself, and when the social worker tried to move her to a new foster home earlier than planned I dug in my heels. If they were going to move her, I wanted it to happen at the last possible minute – I held out hope that her grandmother could get licensed before we left, and that Evie could go straight to her. Until a few days before she was scheduled to be moved, I thought it might happen that way. But in the end, sadly, nothing happened the way that I had hoped. Or even the way that I thought might make this bearable somehow. She was going to a new foster home while her grandmother's licensing process wound its way through the system.

We came to the very last night together. Evie slept in my arms, her body sprawled across mine. Her right hand clutched the underside of my left breast and pressed it to her cheek, while her left hand tugged at my right bra strap. She burped loudly, then wiggled around a bit and fell into a deeper sleep. Watching her, sleeping there on my chest, I begin to worry.

Where was she going to go? Who was going to care for her?

Will they read the letter I tuck in the diaper bag with all the little details about this precious baby?

Will they remember that she sleeps on her side due to her unfortunate habit of projectile vomiting?

Will they care that she prefers the "forest" setting of the sound machine?

Will they buy Huggies because the other diapers gave her a terrible rash?

Will they use the all-natural cornstarch baby powder I packed for her?

Will they dress her in ugly clothes or will they use the cute things I carefully washed and folded in her bag yesterday?

Will they let her sleep on her favorite blanket, with her stuffed toy that smells like me because I've had it on my pillow for three days?

Where will she sleep? Where will she be? Will it be calm and peaceful? Will they love her like I do? How long will she be there?

WHAT IS GOING TO HAPPEN?

All of these thoughts raced around in my mind, jostling for space with the other more rational thoughts like "this isn't your baby" and "you didn't really want to be on a 10 hour plane ride with a teething 7 week old who has a stuffy nose and poops her diaper all day long". Because *I knew* she was not my baby, and I *did* look forward to taking a Xanax and sleeping for at least 9 hours of that 10 hour flight. I did.

My conflict at that point was not about "caring too much" or "getting attached" - foster parents HAVE to care and children need to feel attached. My conflict is that I felt guilty. If I felt this way every time, if

I felt helpless and powerless, if I felt like I was a part of something that was detrimental to a child, I wouldn't foster any more. And while at times the end of a case has been difficult, I am usually convinced that the greater good is being served, and that my role has benefitted the child - I have never before felt the way I did at the end of this case. I have been all manner of annoyed, angry, frustrated, tired, fed up, disgusted horrified and bewildered. But I have never once felt that I was doing less than the very best for the child in my care. And I never wanted to keep the baby forever. Giving her to someone else to raise was just unthinkable.

I felt as though I was abandoning Evie. I felt as though I was not following through on my commitment as her parent - the only custodial parent she had at the moment, and the only parent she had ever known. I was leaving, flying to New England with Max and Lucy for the summer, as we do every year. And I was not taking Evie with me.

I wanted to.

I asked, and then I pleaded.

I wrote emails and made phone calls, all for naught.

After I handed her over to the aide, sound asleep in her carseat, accompanied by the two tote bags full of clothes and blankets that she had accumulated during her short life, I drove home. I tried to will myself to believe that I had done the best for her that I could. That it was out of my hands. After all, her grandmother wanted her, and her grandmother would take care of her and keep her safe. She may be a stranger to Evie, but she was her family. I stayed focused on that thought, of reunifying a family, and how healthy that was for everyone. I put it out of my mind that she was going to go live with strangers in a new foster home for some unknown period of time beforehand, and even when she was transferred to her grandmother she would still be living with strangers - ones to whom she has a biological connection, but with whom she has only spent three or four hours with in an office downtown a month ago. She may stay with them forever, or not. She may eventually have a relationship with her biological mother, or not. They may eventually figure out who her father is, or not. The only thing that I knew for sure is that she wouldn't be with us.

Despite my best intentions, and the stream of encouragement from friends that I was trying to hang on to, it didn't feel right to me. I feel like children should be offered as much continuity as possible. Infants operate almost entirely on the most basic senses - the smell, the touch, the sound of their parent is what bonds them together. So that night, when someone else was tucking her in, I worried that her very little soul would wonder where her mother was.

Who her mother was.

And when she was going to go home.

In the middle of the afternoon I received an email from the social worker that I still had never met, encouraging me to call the new foster parents to tell them about Evie and her routine. They had chosen an older couple to be her foster parents, and the husband would primarily be responsible for her care. Maybe I could give him some support. She also mentioned, very casually, that Evie might not be going to her grandmother after all.

My heart fell. I sat there on the sofa and sobbed. I couldn't speak. I couldn't think about anything other than that they had tricked me. That was how it felt. They had led me on, let me get close, knew that I was attached and that I wanted to keep her until her family could take custody – and now I was being told – in an email – that she might not go to her family, but she couldn't stay with us. As friends called to check in on me, knowing that it was the day she was being moved, I answered the phone choking back tears. I cried for hours.

This was the first time we had found ourselves in this situation - having a child moved from our home to a new foster home against our wishes - and I did not like it one little bit. I have thought a lot about the particulars, about how I came to be in this place at this time, and why it hurt so much. And I think the reason is because Evie was not going to be returned to her family, but returned to the system – and that felt wrong. Terribly wrong, and unjust

She was being shuffled around to another foster home because I was leaving. That is the bottom line. If I had not left Maui for the summer, she could have stayed with me indefinitely. I just couldn't help but feel that it was all my fault. Me and my stupid summer vacation plans. I felt as though I had been irresponsible even taking the case to begin with. I tried to convey my concern to the social worker, and her response told me immediately that I had been labeled a problem. Her email in response to mine was cold, bordering on condescending. Had I been expecting to adopt this child? I had to look at fostering as a job. I had to be prepared to say goodbye, she reminded me.

She expressed concern that I had let myself become attached, but I don't see that as the real problem. I think that you have to become attached to each child, in order for them to feel attached to someone in return; in order for them to feel safe, and capable of giving and receiving love and trust. Parenting is a very symbiotic relationship – each nurtures the other. Closing yourself off to love is not necessarily the healthiest way to get through life. You have to be able to love deeply, and then move on. As a foster parent you cannot forget - not for a moment - that this is someone else's child. But at 3am, when you are cleaning vomit off the wall while whispering sweet nothings to the creature snoring in the Baby Bjorn on your chest, sometimes you forget......and I think that is okay.

Epilogue

When people discover my daughter is adopted, they are always shocked. They ask a lot of questions – the whys and the hows and the "she is so lucky to have found you. It was meant to be."

She is lucky to have found us? No, it is absolutely the other way around. Anyone who has tried – and failed – to conceive can back me up on this. Adoption is the greatest gift any parent could give - or receive. And I have found, through the years, that foster parenting is much the same. Yes, there are differences – huge, mind bending differences - between adoption and foster care. But the feeling that I have when I hold a child in my arms is always the same: everything is as it should be in that moment.

When I tell people we are foster parents, I usually get one of two responses:

The first is total shock. Somehow, my husband and I don't match the pre-conceived notions the general public seems to have about "the kind of people" who become foster parents.

The second response is something along the lines of "I always thought about becoming a foster parent, but (insert various reasons here) I never followed through on it."

With either response there come a lot of questions, which I am always happy to answer. But more importantly, every conversation about foster parenting brings with it an opportunity to encourage others to foster. The system needs safe, loving foster homes. The system needs foster parents who can demonstrate a healthy, happy "normal" home life. And there are so many children out there who need a family to care for them – sometimes just for a little while, and sometimes forever. Many times there are more challenges faced by foster parents then faced by parents who have biological children. Foster parenting is by no means a "trial run" for becoming a parent – you have to be prepared for your heart to swell with love, and to break.

Sometimes simultaneously.

People ask, repeatedly, how I can be a foster parent. More specifically, they want to know how I can stand to give the babies back. That is actually the biggest concern everyone has: "How do you give them back?" they ask. "I would never be able to do that!"
What does that mean, exactly? They 'would never be able to do that'?
I give them back because these babies are not mine. And this is not about me.
I know in my heart that I have raised my babies. Foster children already have a mother and a father, and many times I have met them. We spend time together at doctor's appointments, or communicate when I drop the baby off for visitation. And if I have met them, it means they show up, that they are making their child a priority in their life. And that counts for something.
It means they are trying.

I cannot judge someone who is trying to make amends, turn their life around, and be the best person - and parent - they can be. The parent their child deserves.

In those situations, my job as a foster parent is to help them out, while they help themselves.

I am the surrogate, and the example: I show them how to care for a newborn. Their baby arrives to each visit bathed, dressed in clean clothes, with a stocked diaper bag and a bottle. Their baby travels in a carseat that has straps that fit properly, that is clean and in good repair. Their baby is gaining weight, and responsive, and sometimes even smiling. Their baby goes to checkups regularly, and sees specialists to deal with medical problems associated with fetal drug and alcohol exposure. And for the most part, the parents pay attention to their baby. People ask how I can stand to give the babies back - I wonder how the parents can stand to be away from their babies. I cannot even imagine handing my baby to a complete stranger. I am rooting for them. I want them to succeed, and to have their baby home with them. But sometimes, showing up for a 90 minute supervised visit is the extent of their interest. Raising a baby is not their priority. And at times like that - when the biological family seems to view the baby as an object rather than a person - it is almost impossible to model good behavior. When a parent shows up high, or worse doesn't show up at all, I want to pick up the baby and get back in the car and say "Never mind." They are not trying to help themselves, or their child.

They are not interested in helping anyone.

And I think that is what people are thinking of, when they ask how I can give these babies back. But for the most part *(and yes, there are always exceptions, but for the most part)* babies don't go back to parents until the parents have gone through an exhaustive process to regain custody. If only every parent had to meet these standards before bringing their baby home. Parents who get their kids back from foster care have made some serious effort.

On the other hand, when parents are completely disconnected from the child, when they act as though there is no rush to get their act together, as though the child is a toy to be played with and then put away, when they continue to abuse drugs, when they have no idea what their child weighs, or how to put on a diaper even after seven weeks of visits, when extended family is asked to raise the child and they suggest that maybe they could "just visit the baby instead".......at those times I am not worried about them regaining custody. Instead, I become the mama bear. The gate closes. The smiles and friendly chit chat at visits fades. And I hold the baby closer. Because someone has to. Someone has to hold this baby, put him first, get up with him each night and greet him each morning. Someone has to want to be his mother all the time - not just for 90 minutes a few times a week.

Every child deserves to be someone's priority. Being a foster parent is being the one person in the world who puts this child first. Sometimes because the parents can't. Sometimes because they won't. I have no control over whether they want to be parents, and I can't help people who can't help themselves. All I know is that as long as a baby is with me, that baby is my priority. And that baby is just as important as Max and Lucy. I don't care for these babies when it's convenient. I don't love them part time, I love them all the time. Even at 3am, when I would much rather be sleeping.

And I don't know how anyone could feel any differently.

Carpe Diem, I would say to anyone who asked how I was going to give another baby up. And I believe it. I have to believe that it is better to have loved and lost, than never to have loved at all.

That is not to say that it is easy – it is never easy to say goodbye to a child you have parented. I have recovered, somewhat, from saying goodbye to Evie, but I am sure I have been red flagged at child protective services as a drama queen with attachment issues. I wouldn't change a thing.

 I still believe that things could be different – have to be different - in order for our family to continue to foster children. We have to be able to say goodbye at the end of each case without feeling as though the entire world has been torn apart.

After a lot of contemplation, we have decided that if we are ever asked to take a case and it is clear that we cannot make a long term commitment, then we will not accept the placement. Period. I cannot do it. I have found my line. I have to see each case through to the end, whenever and where ever that might be. That is what every child deserves – love, stability, and continuity. Foster parenting is a different type of parenthood, to be sure; an abbreviated, dense experience full of extremes and immediacy and unknown variables, but it is also full of hope and possibilities the likes of which you may never have imagined. Raising your own child is a challenge. Raising someone else's child is a calling.

"It's not only children who grow. Parents do too. As much as we watch to see what our children do with their lives, they are watching us to see what we do with ours. I can't tell my children to reach for the sun. All I can do is reach for it myself"

– Joyce Maynard

Bringing Home Baby: All You Really Need
(a reasonable, manageable, affordable checklist)

I have told every expectant mother who will listen that they do not need everything that every parenting magazine says they needs. A lot of pressure is put on new parents to buy a bunch of stuff – and they use very convincing words like "safer" and "peace of mind" and "your baby's comfort" and often refer to the "latest guidelines" and "new safety standards". The result is that every prospective parent thinks that – even if they already have a bunch of baby stuff in the attic – they need all new and improved stuff and if they don't get it they will not be doing the very best for their child. It is a cheap shot, in my mind. Of course we all want the best for our children.

But do they really need to have the poop wiped off their bums with a warm wipe, instead of a room temperature one? No. No they do not. I am here to tell you that babies will scream and cry at a diaper change no matter how warm their wipe is.

Don't buy into the hype. The reason second and third and all subsequent children don't get a bunch of new stuff is because many of the things that you think you need end up being totally unnecessary. I have taken care of COUNTLESS newborns, and I can promise that you need very little. Really.

I know this, because I myself totally bought the hype. All of it. Some of it I bought twice. And I regretted it even more the second time. I speak from experience when I tell you: newborn babies need the very basic necessities. They do not need the very latest gadgets. The following is a list of the basics that you should have ready and waiting. You can get more of whatever you need once the baby arrives, this is just what you need to get started.

1. Carseat

Infant car seats have size limits so you may only be able to use them for a year or so -but they are very handy during that time. If there is a possibility you will care for a child over the age of one, skip the infant car seat and get a convertible seat that can be used facing backward and forward. Even if you do not own a car, you need a car seat. Please do not buy a used car seat – if a car seat has been in a car during a car accident it is no longer safe to use. Best to buy new.

2. Stroller

Strollers are optional but extremely useful, and easy to find free or cheap. Ask around, someone may have one to give you. Some strollers allow for an infant car seat to be clipped over the seat. Some recline. Some are super lightweight. All are useful in their own way. If you are using public transportation you want a lightweight, compact one. If you buy a travel system, chances are good that your stroller will be huge and heavy. Mine didn't fit in the trunk of my car. This was a problem.

3. Baby Carrier

Usually referred to by brand name (Snugli, Baby Bjorn, Ergo, etc.) you will appreciate having a carrier - I recommend the Ergo which is heaven on my back. Slings and other front carriers have varying levels of satisfaction, and I have one of each. I have a Bjorn and a sling for the first few months, but as soon as they get heavy, I switch to the Ergo. Babies almost universally want to be carried around, so figure out what works best for you – it will make your days – and nights – easier.

4. **Vibrating seat or swing** this is another not necessary but incredibly useful item for a newborn. A vibrating seat is great for those times when the parent is in the bathroom, doing laundry, cleaning, or trying to type/eat/drink hot beverages. You don't need it, but some sort of seat or swing is nice to have from time to time. And sometimes the baby will fall asleep in it!

5. Bed

You need a place for the baby to sleep. Babies can sleep anywhere, including mangers and laundry baskets. Don't go nuts. Buy a play yard (with a bassinet attachment if you will be caring for a newborn) because they store easily. Have at least two fitted sheets. If you have room for a crib, great – but those have a lot of safety regulations and recalls, so be very careful to buy a crib that meets current guidelines. And skip the quilt and bumper set and decorative pillows - they have been deemed unsafe for sleeping babies

6. Feeding

Burp cloths - we use cotton diapers and hand towels and strips of cotton t-shirts as burp cloths.

Bottles - I have 6 bottles with lids.

7. Bathing

Baby bathtubs are very useful and much safer than the kitchen sink - especially if you are inexperienced – because babies are slippery. So please buy a baby tub for safety. **note**Babies do not need a bath for the first few weeks – definitely not until their belly button is healed. And when it is finally time for that first bath, I prefer the "sling" style bathtub with a mesh seat.

Baby soap is key, you need something completely free of fragrance and preservatives as some babies are very allergic to those things. I suggest Dr. Bronner's Baby soap or California Baby.

Boudreaux Butt Paste. This stuff is miraculous when your baby has a diaper rash.

Petroleum jelly (for circumcision care)

8. Clothes and Blankets Do not buy brand new clothes. Go to Goodwill or yard sales, and take hand-me-downs from friends and neighbors. I recommend having a small supply tucked away in various sizes. We have 3 white snap-crotch t-shirts in every size, a pair of stretchy pants in every size (neutral colors) and a little sweater in every size. The hospital always sends home a hat, but if you live in an area with cold winters, you will need a better hat – not wool, something soft – and a bunting of some sort. You should have several blankets – thin flannel, knit cotton, and a warm fuzzy one. Also, get a large swaddling blanket.

And pull out a tote bag, backpack or large purse to use as a diaper bag.

To buy right before baby comes home:

Nipples new bottle nipples for every baby. You want the smallest size and slowest flow for newborns. Age ranges and flow speed are usually printed on the package.

Formula find out what the baby has been eating, and try to get the exact same kind.

Pacifier I buy one when I buy nipples – rubber can dry out and crack in storage.

Diapers and Wipes Again, some babies have very sensitive skin, so buy wipes for sensitive skin until you know what you are dealing with. Baby boys who have just been circumcised would be better off with cotton balls and warm water until they have healed a bit. Find out how much the baby weighs, and if the baby is right between sizes always go UP a size.

Infant Tylenol

Baby Thermometer

4973427R00133

Made in the USA
San Bernardino, CA
18 October 2013